Indigo Warrior

A Guide for Indigo Adults
& the Parents of Indigo Children

Lisa Andres

Cover Design by Regina Wamba:
http://www.MaeIDesign.com

Editing by Durham Editing and E-books:
http://editingandebooks.com

ISBN: 0-9912394-6-6
ISBN 13: 978-0-9912394-6-7
Library of Congress Control Number: 2014914851

CONTENTS

Lisa Andres

INTRODUCTION

I am a psychic medium. I am an author. I am a singer. I am also an Indigo.

I had no idea what an Indigo was until a few years ago. Like many others that are around New Age reading material or shops and find themselves with like minds, I had heard the term "Indigo" swirl around me in reference to children and never had explored it.

In a class I had for mediums in 2009, the teacher referred to me as "Indigo Warrior." She said, "Hello, Indigo Warrior." I looked behind me, wondering if she was talking to someone else. She wasn't. I shrugged my shoulders, having no idea what that meant, and said hello back to her. Several times during that weekend class, she addressed me as "Indigo Warrior." I made a mental note to look further into what an Indigo was when I got home.

When I later looked into the term "Indigo," I realized that there were not a lot of books out there about Indigos. Most of them are for Indigo children. That drove me to address Indigo adults as well as children in this book. I'm an Indigo adult, and I wanted to share the information that I have learned in the years since I was first addressed as Indigo Warrior.

I was inspired to write this book when listening to a friend of mine as she told me about her daughter's anger. She didn't understand it. She didn't think that she and her husband had done anything as parents to cause the anger, but, like good parents, they still felt responsible. They were starting to wonder how to deal with it. When they told me about one situation, a light bulb went on in my head showing me that her daughter was an Indigo. So I began to arm her with some information.

In my practice as a psychic medium, I started to draw Indigo adults and children to me in my readings. The best thing about what I do is seeing the relief in people who realize that they are finally being understood, to know that they are Indigos and finally have a confirmation of all the things they have been through.

I later had another class with the teacher that had originally called me Indigo Warrior. In that second class, she asked the people that were Indigos to stand. In a crowd of hundreds of people, a handful of us hesitantly stood. She then asked the rest of the audience to give us a round of applause because the Indigos were the people here to help in leading the way for others.

It is my hope in writing some of my experiences with and about Indigos that it helps you. You are very important to the world right now.

CHAPTER 1
WHAT IS AN INDIGO?

An Indigo is a lightworker who was called to Earth as the result of prayers for positive changes to our planet. A lightworker is someone with a global purpose and an individual life purpose. A global purpose is a life purpose that helps others in some way, in addition to themselves. A lightworker may also be known as an Earth Angel. It is called a global life purpose because helping others could extend to a potentially global level.

There was chaos that erupted on Earth in World War I and II. The first large influx of lightworkers in our current generation came to Earth as a result of the prayers for peace and resolution of the Earth's problems. This is better known as the "Baby Boom" of the 1950s. Many of the people from the Baby Boomer generation were the parents of the large influx of adult Indigos.

Indigos are born to bring truth and justice to the world. Many Indigos have a very warrior-like presence. They are born tough. They are often born to speak truth. They have a natural lie detector and can detect inauthentic character in others. They may have been punished at some point in their lives for not being able to hold their tongues.

They are on what seems to be a constant search for truth and justice. They see through the character of others easily and are not patient with character flaws or with someone they don't trust. For instance, if they sense that someone is not exactly what he or she seems, even if Indigos have no proof of it, they trust the sense that something is off about the person. Most other people would give a person they had a bad feeling about a chance, only to learn the hard way. Indigos trust that inner truth detector and honor it right away. They won't give anyone the time of day that they don't trust or have a bad vibe about for any reason. They commonly come without a filter, so to speak, because they represent truth and have a hard time keeping their truth to themselves.

Indigos often wonder why they were dropped off on this planet because they've never felt like they belong. They spend their whole life feeling different, and they may spend time trying to fit in only to realize it doesn't suit them. Indigos are born to be different.

Indigos generally are, or think they are, the smartest people they know. They may not make the best classroom students because they grow impatient and oftentimes think they are smarter than the teacher. Often they already know the information they are being given. They have a tendency to either be asked to skip ahead grades, or they completely flunk out of school or drop out of school because they are frustrated with the entire process.

Patience is not a virtue that is found in abundance in Indigos. They know they have a big life purpose even if they don't know exactly what it is. They have no patience for dishonesty or corruption of any kind. They are born with a huge sense of purpose. They can get frustrated at a young age when they have an inner knowing they are here on Earth for a special mission, but they may not know what that mission is, or have the capacity to execute it, in their young years.

Many Indigos tend to be born into dysfunction of some sort. That may mean dysfunction in the family home or stressful situations in childhood. Many Indigos were, or are, bullied in school.

Indigos may become lawyers to fight laws that no longer serve us. They are soldiers, police officers, or work in some capacity to protect others.

Indigos do not feel like they can fit in a box. Ever. No matter the category, they have never completely fit. That frustrates them, but that is also one of the many things that helps push them towards their life purpose. They break the box and make new categories that fit; in doing so, they lead the way for others.

Indigos have a strong sense of independence. They are natural leaders and want to do things their own way. They have an intense presence, and they will take the command of a room just upon entering it. Some Indigos may be tossed into leadership positions, whether they like it or not. Many Indigos have a tendency to get fired from or lose jobs. Because of this, they are often self–employed and are their own bosses. As a result, many Indigos are entrepreneurs.

Indigos tend to be a handful as children, as they have no shortage of energy. Overall, more than anything, Indigos feel misunderstood. That starts when they are children. They tend to have a lot of energy and don't know what to do with it. They may be put on a medication at some point because those around them can't deal with such intense, restless energy. Indigos might be diagnosed with Attention

Deficit Disorder (ADD), Attention Deficit Hyperactivity Disorder (ADHD), or Post Traumatic Stress Disorder (PTSD).

Many Indigos have a serious look on their faces. They have what some describe as an "old soul" that has experienced its share of pain. Many are asked, "Why do you always look so serious?" One of the reasons for that serious or penetrating look in their eyes is that they are old souls who have seen the destruction and sadness that can happen on Earth many times. They may not come across that way, but the depth in the experience of their soul, whether in this lifetime or others, knows that life is serious and heavy. It's one of the things Indigos are here to help others with: the heaviness of Earth when things need to change. They inherently know they are here for an important mission.

The injustices of Earth upset these lightworkers. Indigos may be pet rescuers, people rescuers, law changers, charity founders, and more. They are the whistle blowers. They want justice and won't stop until they get it.

Indigos have a tendency to be tattooed, pierced, emo, Goth, or anything else that expresses their discontent and need to be understood. They are quite familiar with curse words and use them regularly. It's not that they don't know how to speak properly; it's just that they have to honor their truth at any price. Making people uncomfortable is something Indigos seem to be good at, so at some point they just learn to go with the flow of that and express themselves in whatever way they see fit.

The bottom line is this: Indigos are here to help people, young or old. Indigos have no set age. Many adult Indigos were born in the 1970s, but you can be older than that and still be an Indigo. My grandmother believes that she is an Indigo. There is a large influx of Indigo children that have been born in the last forty years, and it is not going to stop any time soon. I am one of those Indigos, so I can personally relate to many of these characteristics.

Like so many Indigos, I was bullied in school for much of my childhood. I was often punished as a child for not being able to hold my tongue. As an adult, I was thrust into a leadership role. In my career in corporate America, I found out my boss was leaving one day, and I took over managing the team for him the next.

We, as Indigos, are here to pave the way for others, to lead by example, to show others the way. Even if we have no idea how to do that, or that we are even doing it, we often set an example just in our very being. We stand for truth, and whether we present as a bad boy, a smart girl, or whatever it may be, our very presence demands attention. People can't help but notice, and we set an example because of it. Others need our help or for us to show them the way by doing whatever it is that we are good at. We are truth. We are leaders. We are honest. We are angry. We want justice. We will stop at no cost to do what's right.

This world needs Indigos. It needs you or your child that is an Indigo. You have not lived your life for nothing. You have not been abused or felt like you didn't fit in for nothing. You were incarnated for this time to help others. You are not alone, even if you have felt like it your whole life.

You are a warrior.

You are beautiful.

You are an Indigo.

CHAPTER 2
HOW DO I KNOW IF I AM AN INDIGO?

Traits of the Indigo:

- Wise, expressive eyes
- Warrior-like presence
- Truth-speaking
- Justice-seeking
- Intelligent
- Angry
- Powerful
- Sharp tongue
- Impatience
- Prone to addiction
- Often diagnosed as ADD, ADHD, PTSD

Have you always felt you've been misunderstood? Like maybe you were dropped off on the wrong planet or were just in the wrong family? Do you feel like you have had to constantly apologize for who you are? Or that your energy is too intense for others to be around? Have you had times when you just wished you were more normal? Have you ever been referred to as "a bull in a china shop" or something similar?

You have always felt like the different one, and, in many instances, the family you grew up in made it abundantly clear that you were different from them, which lead to feeling isolated even more.

You've always been a leader, whether you wanted to be or not. You are somehow always nominated to be the boss, or you just plain enjoy being the boss. You certainly could not handle anyone being your boss. You might have been fired a time or two because you could not take being told what to do for one minute longer. Now, you are your own boss, and that suits you well. If you haven't been a formal leader, you've been a leader in some way, even if it was just paving the way for others by taking the first step on an unknown road.

You have often been told that you look too serious, or too mean, or that you should "smile more." You might be tattooed and pierced because it's the best way you can express yourself. Maybe you have even dyed your hair pink just to stand out. You were aware long ago that you always stand out whether you like it or not, so you do it on your own terms.

You had a hard time in school; you might have had a learning disability or just a general impatience for the school and teachers. Sometimes you felt smarter than the teacher; that may have led to you either leaving school or transitioning to a different school that better fit your needs.

You're not a stranger to a fight, but you are not always looking for one. You fight, or have fought, to protect yourself or people around you. It might even be your job to protect others in some way.

You have a hard time keeping your opinion to yourself. You have been told that you need a filter on your mouth or need to learn how to shut your mouth. You can sense the character of another person at first sight and have little patience for small talk. The injustices of the world make you mad.

You like your cigarettes, alcohol, caffeine, or other vices. If this is not a current habit, it could have been one in the past that you have overcome.

You have a past that you don't like to tell people about because you don't want them to pity you. Your childhood was dysfunctional and abusive: physically, verbally, or both. You may have been sexually abused or raped at some point. You may have been told you were imagining the abuse when you tried to tell an adult. You may have been in abusive relationships as an adult. Injustice in this world makes you MAD. You cannot stand to see someone abused or treated unfairly.

You've always felt frustrated. You have no idea why. Frustration bubbles inside you at knowing you have a higher purpose but now knowing what that purpose is.

You could not blend in if you tried. You have wished to be normal but never felt normal. You have wished to not be noticed as easily as you are. You have been told your energy is harsh or powerful as if you are doing something wrong in just being. You have felt rejected in many ways, like a misfit of sorts. You have never truly felt that you fit in.

You may have a history of relationship problems. You may be divorced—maybe more than once. You may have moved or changed residences more than is comfortable for you. You may have moved from state to state, or country to country, because you felt called somewhere, only to find yourself right back where you started, and you don't understand why.

You sometimes wonder if you were sent to Earth to be alone. You'd rather be alone than be in a relationship that makes you wish you were alone.

Some days the world feels too heavy. You easily feel like you absorb the heavy energy of crowds. You wonder what on Earth you did to deserve to be here because you know somehow that your soul wouldn't have—couldn't have—chosen this. At the very least, you know you had to be asked to come down to Earth to help others because you couldn't have done it willingly.

If you nodded your head in agreement, and perhaps shed a tear, when reading some or all of these statements, you are indeed an Indigo.

I'm so relieved to have found you and that you have found me.

You are not alone.

CHAPTER 3
CHARACTER TRAITS OF INDIGOS

<u>Vocal</u>

Indigos are born without filters on their mouths. I can't tell you how many times I've heard someone say to me that he or she doesn't have a filter. Whenever I hear that now, I know that the person I'm being told about is probably also an Indigo. I recently met someone who informed me that she did not have a filter. I laughed, knowing that person was probably an Indigo.

As Indigos, we are also born to know truth. When we sense that things are not truthful, we point them out. We have opinions, can't stand to see injustices, and are the first to call someone out on something that we perceive as unjust. Not all Indigos are extremely vocal. Some may be quiet or observers. But when they have something to say, watch out. They don't talk unless they have to, and then they don't quiet down easily.

By saying Indigos' words are often unfiltered, I mean that we don't typically think about what we are going to say before we say it. We spill out our opinions or truths, regardless of how these might hurt or offend the person we are talking to.

I didn't have a filter until I had a job that forced one on me. When I became a manger in corporate America, I learned quickly that I would have to learn how to "talk the talk" and "walk the walk." I used to wonder why there wasn't an unofficial handbook for managers that included in it the language managers should use to be effective. It was hard at first, but gradually it instilled a filter in me both in and outside of work. At least the filter works most of the time.

Indigos are direct. We don't mince words. We don't mean to offend anyone with our sharp tongue. It's just that Indigos believe in truth, and anything else is unimportant. Older indigos may have had many experiences being scolded, slapped across the face, or having their mouths washed out with soap as kids because they just could not seem to control their words even if they knew they'd be punished. Most Indigos don't think about what we are going to say long enough to consider the consequences. We talk first and think about what we said later, and that's only if we have to.

Impatient

Patience is not usually a normal virtue of an Indigo. We were born impatient. It was like we know we have a purpose that is bigger than us and can't wait for it to begin or to figure out what that purpose is.

We have a tendency to lose our tempers rather quickly when our patience is being tested, and, as children, that can bring out the worst in us. As children, we seriously test our parents, and impatience often escalates to tantrums and episodes that our parents don't know what to do with.

As adults, everything Indigos have to do has to be done yesterday. We are all about action steps. When there's not an action step to take, we become impatient. We may form nervous habits like cracking our knuckles to signal our impatience.

One thing that most of us are impatient with is small talk. We simply don't have time for preamble and niceties when it's the heart of the matter, the truth of things, we are trying to get to. We don't want to waste time with fluff when we feel that what we are saying or doing should have a point. We are skeptical of someone who tries to talk too much about the weather or something else when we have no interest in it.

Excellent Judges of Character

Indigos always know whether we will like someone just by sensing their energy. We tend to make good police officers or tend to be in similar professions where we have to make intuitive decisions about the character of another person. We may walk into a place and say we don't like the way it feels and insist upon leaving immediately. We are like this with people, too. We may have a sense of uneasiness or know that a person is not who we want to be around. If it's your child that is the Indigo, they might try to tell you about this feeling concerning another person. You may shush or punish your child for saying this, only to later discover that your child was right when the person they were trying to tell you about hurts you.

Intense

Indigos have a fierce look of intensity in our eyes. Even when we mean to smile, it might look to someone else like we are mad at them. We have a penetrating look in our eyes as if we can see into the souls of others. And sometimes we can. We walk into a room and couldn't blend in if we tried. The ferocity of our energy just seems to precede us as we enter a room. People either look at us like they're trying to figure us out, or they look down because we intimidate them.

Indigos are often asked, "Would you calm your energy down?" I was even asked that once by another psychic medium. It was almost as if the person reading me was frustrated at my powerful energy field. This person then proceeded to tell me that I had to work on toning my energy down so I wouldn't have as harsh of an impact when I enter a room. Sometimes our energy is so big we notice light bulbs mysteriously go off or break when we are near. I have had this happen too many times to be a coincidence.

Indigos know we couldn't be normal if we tried, so most of us stopped trying long ago. I remember once being scolded by one of my bosses for my harsh demeanor. I told him I would try the best I could but that it might be difficult for me to be someone that I'm not. I've grown tired of apologizing to other people for who I am because my very energy, or attitude, offends them.

Sensitive

Indigos are beautifully sensitive people. At times, it can feel like we absorb the sadness of Earth. When we hurt, it impacts us on a very deep level. We may become guarded as a result of that. Underneath the invisible walls that we tend to build around ourselves is a depth of vulnerability that makes us very sensitive. As a result of that, sometimes we get defensive. Our tempers spark easily. What lies beneath that is a sensitivity that is so pure that sometimes we don't know what to do with it. That, in turn, can make our emotions feel heavy.

CHAPTER 4
PORTRAIT OF AN INDIGO

The Indigo Child

When I do readings for parents of Indigo children, they come into the reading not knowing the answer they are looking for or the term that fits their child. They just know that they have a child that is different and want to know more about it.

As parents, I can only imagine that you feel that all of your children are special in many wonderful ways. Indigo children are usually the ones that challenge you the most. They are usually the children that you can't control or seem to get to behave no matter what you do.

They may have sudden bouts of anger and become frustrated easily. They usually get bored, seem impatient, and don't seem to know how to quell those feelings. As such, the anger they have can manifest into behaviors that are disruptive, not only to your child but to the rest of your family. They may have been diagnosed, or possibly even misdiagnosed, as having ADD or ADHD. If it's not a typical diagnosis, they still may be on some form of medication to subdue their extra energy or anger.

Indigo children tend to have an endless supply of energy. It can be a good thing, but it can be a highly frustrating thing for a parent when the child never settles down. They are born with a knowing that they have a higher purpose, and I believe that knowing is within their soul and manifests as endless energy. This can also manifest into anger. I write about the anger inherent in the Indigo, and that starts when they are very young.

My best friend's daughter always had endless energy. I know that my friend and her husband were great parents. There were no other children in their home to upset their child, but, as parents, they didn't understand why she always seemed so angry.

One night my friend told me that her then-10-year-old daughter had publicly called another child "stupid," and they had punished her as a result. At that moment, the Indigo within me regressed to my own similar childhood moments. Moments where, as a child, I felt unjustly punished. It may not have been appropriate for the girl to call another child "stupid," but an Indigo speaks his or her truth. That was probably her truth at the moment she said it. She just could have said it a bit better. In hearing that, I felt like that had been the story of my life as I was growing up.

Indigos tend to not have a filter on their mouths, and I don't have to tell you that most children don't have filters. With an Indigo, that is escalated. Indigos are born to speak truth and know the truth before most other people. They will tell you about someone's character, and they are probably right whether you realize that or not.

Some Indigo children may have a hard time in school.

They might even get kicked out of school. That is not because they are dumb by any stretch of the imagination. They are just frustrated with the entire learning process. They either feel they are smarter than the teacher or just plain don't have time for school. Some Indigos are prone to learning disabilities which may inhibit their learning in a traditional school environment.

If you have an Indigo child in your home, it may be the one that you are punishing frequently for acting up in some way. You may feel that this child threatens other children in your home in some way. That is not always the case, but it is definitely possible with an Indigo in the home. If you are the parent of an Indigo, you are probably frustrated. You might even feel at your wit's end with your child. You have tried everything and don't know what else to do.

It is also possible that you have a child that meets one or more of these qualities I described but not all of them. Perhaps your child has a more gentle energy most of the time but is prone to sudden outbursts of anger that escalate beyond what you would consider normal.

If you identify with this, it is possible that you have an Indigo child. I must admit that I am not a parent, but in my research and speaking to other parents of Indigo children, I've come up with some suggestions that may help.

Diet

The diet of any child is very important. Indigo children are more susceptible to hyperactivity as a result of the foods that they eat. As a parent, try to be conscious of not letting them have too much sugar, caffeine, or any other stimulant that can take the excess energy of an Indigo and escalate it. Indigo children would also benefit from having as much natural, fresh food in their diet as possible. They are very sensitive to the chemicals and additives found in processed foods.

Anger Outlets

A great outlet for the anger of an Indigo child is physical activity. This may be a traditional sport like basketball or soccer, or it could be something like going to a karate class. It can also be through an activity such as playing a musical instrument or singing. When I was a child, I liked to sing. I would play my records and sing to the top of my lungs. I had no idea it was an outlet for my natural Indigo anger, but it was.

I watched an interview on Oprah's Master Class with Alicia Keys about growing up in a rough neighborhood. Her mother scheduled her after-school activities to keep her so busy that she didn't have time to get into trouble. While I am not saying that Alicia Keys is an Indigo or not, this would be a good practice for any parent wanting to keep their child focused, such as the parent of an Indigo.

Empowerment

Find a way to empower your Indigo child. Indigos are natural born leaders. Find a way to give your child a voice. Indigos are children that need to feel that they have a voice. They need to feel heard. They need to make a difference.

Indigos are also lightworkers. Lightworkers are on Earth to help other people in addition to themselves. Is there a way that you can involve your child with a volunteer project of some sort? You might take them to an animal shelter to give the pets there some attention while the pets wait for their forever home, send a letter to a soldier, or help raise money for other students in need. There are many possibilities based on what the child would like to do and what works for your family.

Create an Environment of Understanding

Overall, more than anything, Indigos feel misunderstood. That starts when Indigos are children. They tend to have a lot of energy and don't know what to do with it. As a result, Indigo children may be diagnosed with ADD or ADHD. They may be put on a medication because those around them can't deal with their heavy, restless energy. Indigo children have a bright light energetically; the drugs dim that light for a time.

These children are independent thinkers that experience extreme highs and extreme lows. They are precocious and often have a very high intelligence level. They may experience some of their hyperactivity in the classroom as a result of being bored with the course work. These are children that have the capacity to learn, even though they may experience a learning disability. That and other challenges that may arise in the classroom will frustrate this child, and they may start to disrupt the classroom as a result.

Together, you and your family may have to work to find creative, firm solutions for your Indigo child. They are little lightworkers that know they are here to do something special, and that starts in childhood.

CHAPTER 5
BAD DREAMS, FEARS, AND THE INDIGO CHILD

Every child has fears and bad dreams. Indigo children are sometimes plagued by them. This goes back to the idea that Indigos are very empathic, meaning that they tend to not only feel their own emotions, but the emotions of others. This expands their fears.

Fear is linked closely with anxiety. I interpret that to mean that somehow our bodies are in dissonance with our souls. Our soul might know our true purpose, and that can scare the human part of us. To me, the souls with the biggest purpose are sometimes the ones with the biggest fears. Regardless, it is normal for an Indigo Child to have disrupted sleep patterns and feel terrified when they are young.

When I was a child, I used to have terrible nightmares. I felt like there were eyes staring at me all the time. I felt like there was some unseen force (a bad force) that was in the room with me. Sometimes I would have dreams that I was lost, and I couldn't wake up; I would feel like I wanted to wake up but somehow could not make myself do it. That scared the living daylights out of me. Whether it was a monster I was dreaming about, the devil (my Roman Catholic upbringing insured that I knew all about hell), or some other creature of my mind, I would always run to my parents' room crying in the middle of the night. That I was a little medium and just didn't know it only added to the anxiety. I always sensed spirits around. I know now that I wasn't imagining it, but it scared the daylights out of me at the time. I told my family the things I saw; paired with that and the continual bad dreams, I was sent to a psychiatrist as a young girl. The psychiatrist tried to tell me that the boogie man wasn't real. But it wasn't the boogie man that was haunting me in my dreams. I used to stand on my bed in the middle of the night as if somehow that would protect me from all the spirits I thought were after me.

Your Indigo child may experience something similar. The Indigos that are coming to Earth now are more evolved souls who also may be telling you that they see or talk to dead people, angels, or other supernatural beings. It's important to a little Indigo to feel listened to. Whether or not you believe your child, whether or not you have had enough of what you consider to be your child's nonsense, try your best to let your scared, little Indigo have a voice. He or she came here with a huge life purpose, and your child is likely afraid of all that pressure on his or her soul. Perhaps your child is afraid of all the things that his or her soul knows that your child hasn't yet realized.

I believe that, before we come to Earth, we work with God to plan our lives. Then we are sent to Earth. Our souls may be wise and evolved, but when we come to Earth as babies, our memories of those past lives are taken from us. It's our job on Earth to remember what our soul truly knows, but the process of doing so tends to cause us anxiety and heightens our fears.

If you have a child with night terrors, nightmares, or heightened sensitivity that you don't know what to do with, ask your angels for help. We all have angels that are with us that want to help. The trick is to ask. They can't intervene unless we ask them. Archangel Metatron is the archangel that works with Indigo children. You don't have to remember that name; just pray for help, and, if you think of it, ask the angels for help. Their help comes to you in the form of ideas and thoughts and may come in ways that you don't expect.

You can also try to talk to your child's *oversoul*—that's another term for the higher self. Tell your child that he or she is safe. Sometimes the reason why a child screams the minute it comes from its mother's womb is because to be in a human body is to be away from the energy that is God. The overwhelming peace and unconditional love that we feel when we are with Him in Heaven is suddenly taken from the child. Then we come to Earth and are attached to a body once again, and that feeling disappears. That scares us even as adults and may be a part of why your child is so distressed.

CHAPTER 6
THE EARLY YEARS OF AN ADULT INDIGO

As I explained earlier, adult Indigos often had difficult childhoods. There are many reasons that may have happened, but one reason is that adult Indigos need the rage over being abused, whether physically, emotionally, or verbally, to help them with their life purpose.

There was a large influx of the now-adult Indigos born in the 1970s. I'm not trying to isolate any other adult Indigo, but rather address those of you that resonate with this. You could have been born in 1969 or 1980 and still be in the group I'm addressing. If this feels like it fits and you technically were not born in the 1970s, this also applies to you.

I was born in the United States of America on June 18, 1972. It was a heavy time on Earth. There was war in Vietnam. The political scandal now known as Watergate resulted in an impeachment trial and the later resignation of U.S. President Richard Nixon. It wasn't too long after the "Make Love, Not War" movement started, as well as

Woodstock.

Shortly before I was born, my parents moved across the country from upstate New York to Minnesota, roughly 1,100 miles. It was the same country but a different region of the country, and there were some cultural differences. The stress I was born into started when I was in the womb. I was an unplanned pregnancy to a teenager. My mom was 18, but my parents were unmarried. They said they used three forms of birth control and still got pregnant. I think that means I was supposed to be here. My parents were divorced before I can remember.

As a young child, I lived in a neighborhood where I was bullied. After a while, I had to learn to physically fight to defend myself. I was beat-up by everybody, or so it felt. I remember one day even a boy punched me in the stomach more times than I care to count. I was about 12 or 13 when that happened.

Indigos tend to feel isolated; this goes back to that childhood knowing that we are different. We've always been different, and no one understands this. Many adult Indigos have been through abuse that most people only think exists in books or movies. We wish it only existed there, and we don't like to talk about it. We don't want to bring back those feelings or feel the shame that comes up with them. Most of all, we don't want the pity of others.

I am not a victim of my childhood and neither are you. We survived the abuse, and it made us stronger. It filled us with rage: rage at the people that abused us; rage at the people that allowed it; and rage at the world in general. We don't know what we're doing here, why we had to endure such things, and how we could possibly help anyone else with what we've endured.

All that you have experienced in your life has served a

purpose. The anger you've had bubbling for as long as you remember propelled you to what is ultimately your life purpose. That's the anger that makes you furious when others suffer. You feel that anger because you know that there are things that need to change, and, if no one else is going to change it, you are.

We have arrived at the time in history when it is our turn to lead the way. There's nothing more important than you and the fact that you have a purpose in leading the way for others. Only you can know the path you are supposed to take in leading others. If you don't know what it is yet, chances are you will discover this.

CHAPTER 7
CRYSTAL CHILDREN

There are other lightworkers besides Indigos. One such group is Crystals. I am including this extra chapter to help those of you that have heard this term or find that your child, or you, may not quite fit into the Indigo category. I have had clients who have also asked me about Crystal children and will include a brief synopsis of Crystals as a result. I do not plan on writing anything further about Crystals as of this writing, which is why I'm including this in this book.

To me, Crystal children are almost the antithesis of Indigo children. This doesn't mean that they are the enemy of the Indigo, but rather that all lightworkers have different life purposes and are here to ultimately make the world a better place. Crystal children are lightworkers, too. They are sensitive souls who internalize what they feel whereas Indigos often externalize what they feel.

Crystals tend to have big, expressive eyes. They may not speak right away. These are the children that are sometimes diagnosed with developmental delays like

Autism or Asperger's Syndrome as a result of that.

If you are the parent of Crystal children, you may have to take extra time and patience with them in teaching them to speak in their early years. They may rest their forehead against yours often, especially in their years of not talking. Their souls remember a time when you could communicate telepathically. When they touch their forehead to yours, they are trying to speak through their and your third eyes. Third Eye is an esoteric term that refers to our inner eye. It is in the center region of your forehead.

Crystal children tend to have a connection to nature. They may want to be outside a lot. If they can't be outside, or are in artificial light often, they tend to get cranky. They may be eco-conscious early in their life, making it a priority to recycle and do things that are kind to the Earth and encouraging the rest of their family to do so.

Crystal children also tend to love animals. You may see this naturally in the interactions that your pets have with a Crystal child in your home. If you don't have pets, this child will want one. When you are in nature, you tend to see a connection between your child and the animals and insects.

These children are not quick to want or find conflict. They are the peace makers in your home or at least want to be. If you have other children, the Crystal child tends to be the relaxed peacemaker in the group.

These children are highly sensitive and empathic. That means that they have the tendency to pick up the emotions of other people. They may cry or emote easily when they imagine the hurt of someone else. They are also highly psychic.

Crystal children are afraid of missing something. They tend to want several sources of information around them. They may be good with technology very early, and they may want to have the computer going and television on in order to have as much information at one time as possible.

Crystal children's life purpose is to open our hearts. They tend to only want to talk to other people who have their hearts open. They tend to be born into peaceful, loving families as a result of that.

CHAPTER 8
ANGER, FRUSTRATION, AND THE INDIGO

For the Indigo adult or child, frustration and anger are a natural part of our being. As I've discussed previously, many of us had childhoods or experiences in our past that naturally fostered our anger. Even if we come from completely functional, loving homes, we are prone to anger.

As Indigos, we are born with a huge sense of purpose. As soon as we can speak and maybe even before that, we voice our frustration. We want to feel important, like we matter and have a voice that can be heard. It's hard for us to find empowerment as children and young adults. When we don't find it, our anger escalates and we don't know what to do with it.

As Indigos age, we tend to feel frustrated, especially when we are not working on our purpose. Many of us don't even know what that purpose is, but we are still frustrated because we know that somewhere in our being there's something we should be doing. Not knowing what that is makes us feel angry.

Someone lying to us or accusing us of something we didn't do enrages us. This goes hand-in-hand with our abhorrence of injustice. I also believe our frustration is something that many of us carry over from past lives where we were wrongly accused of being a heretic or source of evil for the gifts that we had in those lifetimes.

Sometimes Indigos feel like life is so serious or heavy when we think about all that is wrong with the world. This heaviness frustrates us. Everything is a problem that needs a solution, or there's always something to fix. In reality, maybe everything is not as complicated as we tend to think it is. I essentially do math for a living in my day job, working on splitting assets for beneficiaries in financial accounts. It was not something I aspired to do for a career. One day, I jokingly asked my guides what kind of karma was I serving for, having to do all this math all day long. They said to me, "Lisa, it's not karma. You do this math because you CAN. That is all." Life is meant to be simple, even if we think it's not.

Maybe all of this is not what you want to hear, but it is the life of an Indigo. We have an internal sense of anger and frustration that keeps us focused in the direction of our life purpose. We may see things as a problem that need solving, but, ultimately, it's up to us to learn how to manage.

For me, my entire childhood was filled with frustration. Even as I grew and moved away from my parent's home, I continued to feel frustrated. In my late teen years and early to mid-twenties, I was plagued with anxiety. I worried about anything and everything. In those days, AIDS was a new and very real epidemic in the world. I worried about AIDS, getting cancer, you name it. I even worried that the world would end. I spent a year on an antidepressant at one point.

I know now that underlying all that anxiety was the frustration that I was not living my life's purpose. At the time, I thought my life purpose was playing music (I sing and play piano) and sharing it with the world. That was before the days of reality shows such as American Idol or the like, and I had no idea how to get myself out there and play music beyond my bedroom. I later went to school to perform music and ended up in a local cover band for a few years. Imagine my disappointment when the frustration didn't go away after I was finally doing what felt like my life purpose.

I'm a medium. I always knew that there were dead people around me and spent more time than I care to admit trying to block them out or to figure out how to make the dead people go away. That was a source of great anxiety to me because it escalated as I got older, starting in my early twenties. By my early thirties, the feeling that there were dead people all around me and in my house was at a fever pitch. It was frustrating beyond anything else in my life. I felt like I was cursed and didn't know how to make it stop.

Finally, I decided to learn about being a medium. I didn't want to, but I started to feel my choices were limited and that it couldn't hurt. The rest is pretty much history because that led me to a huge piece of my life purpose: being a medium and helping others connect with their loved ones on the other side. It wasn't until I sat down to give readings to others that I realized that being a medium was a talent that I could use in service to others. That helped quiet my frustration. For a while.

When it was time for me to write my first book *Gifted – A Guide for Mediums, Psychics & Intuitives*, the frustration started to increase again. I knew that there was something I was supposed to be doing, but I did not know what it was. I had felt guided to write a book, but it seemed a daunting task, and I'd never really explored it beyond that. What I did know at that time was that the things I used to do that sated me, such as watching the television after a long day of work and having a snack while I did so, now frustrated me. I would squirm with anger instead of enjoying relaxing and watching TV.

When I finally did sit down to write my book, I did so with purpose. Soon I started to notice that every time I wrote the book the frustration was replaced with a sense of peace. Since then, I have written three books, and this is my fourth. The frustration is still there. I feel like there's always a book to write. When I'm not writing, I'm frustrated. When I sit down to write, I'm also frustrated because in the back of my mind I think that there's something else I could be doing. I have to force myself to write, but once I do, I have the peace that I was looking for to begin with.

Still, it's not a perfect system. I, like many of you, have several things I feel are my life purpose. I have wanted a child for most of my adult life. My second marriage ended because I could not become pregnant. I still have this feeling in my soul like I'm supposed to be a mother, and I'm not sure how that's going to happen. Maybe I'll adopt a child. Still, it frustrates me because I can't access the esoteric information inherent within me that could tell me why I'm having this experience. It's the one thing I truly cannot control. It's caused me lots of frustration and grief.

I now realize that frustration is a safe feeling to me. I don't like it, yet it's familiar to me. When I feel that frustration, it's my soul's way of saying that there's something I should be doing, and, like a problem that I have to solve, I have to figure out what it is that I should be doing to make the feeling of frustration go away.

There are days when I'm in my car on the way to work and I feel frustrated. It's a half-hour commute to a day job that I would rather not have. I think to myself that I'm just having a very "Indigo" day, turn the radio up loud, and keep driving. Some days there's nothing else I can do but just feel it and move on.

As Indigos, it's part of our very essence to have frustration. The anger and frustration we feel ultimately drives us to our life purpose, even if we are unsure of what that is.

CHAPTER 9
INDIGOS AND LIFE PURPOSE

The purpose of an Indigo usually revolves around leadership and justice. The injustices of the world make the Indigo angry. We cannot stand to see anyone treated unfairly or abused. We are often police officers, soldiers, or some form of protectors—whether it's in an official capacity or not.

As an Indigo, part of my life purpose is to protect animals. When I was a little girl, I had one cat and one dog. I later developed allergies to them, and both pets had to be taken away. It broke my heart. The minute I was on my own, I got a cat and have had cats ever since. In 2006, I met my cat Mia and instantly fell in love with her. We spent almost six years together. Sadly, I had to put her to sleep on November 11, 2011, because of a longtime illness she'd had, but loving her changed my life for the better. It made me want to help other animals in need.

When I got Mia, I noticed that she was from a rescue organization. I was always so grateful for them having rescued Mia that I started sending them donations when I could. This eventually evolved in me being a volunteer for them. Now I do everything from foster cats—which is how I ended up with three cats, so I keep my fostering limited now—to clean their cages at local pet stores that sponsor the rescue cats. Last fall, I even did my first rescue. A few days before Halloween, I saw an ad on the internet advertising free black kittens. . I was livid. I thought, "Don't these people know that the kittens could be tortured, snake food, or worse if they are free? Someone has to DO something."

Still, I brushed it off. I decided I couldn't save all the cats all the time and said a prayer for them. The next day, the same kittens were still available. In a private group on Facebook for the rescue I volunteer with, I posted the ad and asked if we could rescue them if I could temporarily foster them. I have to add that it was the sixth game of the World Series, and my baseball team, the Boston Red Sox, was in it. I love watching sports so much that I had gone out of my way to get dinner ready early so that all I had to do was come home from work, plop myself down on the couch, and watch my team win. But there I was, driving two hours out of my way to get the last kitten and his mother from the auto shop that had been kind enough to give them shelter. I was still able to catch most of the ball game, and all was well. I would still miss the last game of the World Series if it meant saving the life of an animal in need.

The only reason the auto shop gave me the cats, they said, was because our rescue was "no kill," meaning that it does not euthanize due to overpopulation of animals. When I got there, there was an older kitten they hadn't told me about. I groaned internally but agreed to take the extra kitten, Justin, anyway. Justin was a bit older, so the kittens had presumably been from different litters. For a few weeks, I housed Justin and his mother and little baby brother. That "surprise" kitten later ended up being a part of my family. A few days after I gave the cats to the rescue organization, I adopted Justin.

Since Mia passed in 2011, I have adopted four other cats, three of them from the rescue from which I adopted Mia and for which I volunteer. One of the cats I adopted, Dinah, had been a long time resident of the shelter, having been there for two and a half years. When I got home and saw that on her paperwork, I cried for her and in gratitude that the rescue was no kill and would give her a home for as long as she needed it. I got my cat Parker a few months later because Dinah seemed like she wanted a buddy, and he, too, had been at the rescue for over a year. Dinah only lived for about a year and a half after I got her, but I like to think that the last thing I gave her in life was the home filled with unconditional love she needed. Now I have three cats and sometimes overextend myself volunteering, but I'm happy knowing that I am able to help animals in need.

Indigos tend to have a multifaceted life purpose. Very rarely in life do we have one life purpose. Remember: we are lightworkers which means that we have a global life purpose to help others in addition to living our own life. Think about the things that are important to you in your own life, say, for instance, music.

I grew up playing music. I received my first piano when I was three, and I remember that, at the time, I was always frustrated that I could not read the music in my Little Golden Book full of church hymns. I think my family just got it for me because they thought it was cute; my higher self thinks that perhaps they knew that somehow I needed that instrument. I always liked to sing, too, and played my favorite records and sang along with them. That evolved into my playing the clarinet for a while and, later, into music school in college. I was most passionate about singing, but where I went to school they didn't allow singers to graduate without being able to accompany themselves. It was there that my piano-playing skills—which were mostly self-taught—propelled me into later playing keys and singing in a band.

For a while, I thought that was what I wanted to do for a living, but that later changed. Still, I love music and was in a cover band part-time on the weekends for a few years. I try to go see music whenever I can, and even though I am not actively performing anymore, it doesn't mean I won't. It was and still is a part of my life purpose. For any of us that are performers or entertainers—whether we do that part- or full-time—we expel an energetic vibration as our music touches the people that listen to us or watch us when we perform . I use music to help me blow off some steam; when I have a moment of frustration just like any other Indigo, sometimes I sing to the top of my lungs and, in doing so, channel the excess energy through my voice. I have been doing that all of my life and didn't realize when I was young that it was a naturally built-in activity to purge my excess anger, among other things.

Indigos are natural leaders whether we realize it or not. When I started my life in my adult career in the corporate workforce, I was always a good performer because I liked the job and it gave me a sense of purpose. One day my boss announced he was leaving and I got tossed into the leadership role. It was uncomfortable for me. There was part of me that liked it, and part of me that didn't. I spent the first six months wondering whether or not I could swallow the corporate expectations. Now I've been a manager for 10 years, leading various teams of between 3 to 25 employees at one time. That is a very natural Indigo progression into leadership. Sometimes we end up being leaders whether we want to or not. We're good at it, and others can see potential in us. Many Indigos don't like to have bosses and are self-employed. That is a way to be a leader as well. We will talk more about these types of situations in the careers section of this book.

I have always loved Real Estate. I watch house-flipping shows and read books about flipping houses. I have been studying it for years. My entire family has worked with houses in some way, whether it was as a contractor or as an interior designer. I know it is part of my life purpose in some way, even if I haven't figured out what that is yet. It dawned on me that with the U.S. mortgage crisis over the last fifteen years there were many dilapidated houses, and someone that makes the home livable is healing the house, whether intentionally or not. These people who work on dilapidated homes are improving the value of a neighborhood, and that raises the vibration in many ways. It makes sense to me on that level, and I love it. I haven't done it yet, but I always say that I will flip at least one house before I leave this Earth. Who knows if that will turn into more? But I know that I have had a feeling that I should do that consistently for more than five years, and it won't go away.

If you have a feeling like that—a feeling that won't go away—then you should listen to it. Say, long ago you wanted to be a nurse but, for whatever reason, never pursued it. Now you have a family, and time has gone by. You have no idea how you will ever find the time or money to go to school. If you still think about it consistently, even if it's to push the thought away again, it's still likely part of your life purpose, whether you do it or not.

A life purpose can be simple, or it can be difficult. As we've discussed, Indigos are all about truth and justice. Whistle blowers that expose the illegal activity or injustice of a corporation or organization, sacrificing their jobs and risking prosecution, are honoring a part of their life purpose when they expose the information they have for the benefit of others. They are Indigos that lead the way for others.

I often listen to Hay House Radio (http://www.hayhouseradio.com). In one of their ads between shows, they sometimes feature key note speeches from one of their events. In one of these clips, one of the radio personalities was talking about how when he was a child that women weren't allowed to vote. In further comments about how the world has changed, he implied that in life we follow the rules. When the rules don't make sense, we need to change them. Indigos are the leaders that tend to lead the charge to do something like change a rule or a law, whether big or small.

One main life purpose of any Indigo is to overcome challenges that are natural in the life of the Indigo, and that is putting it lightly. Another part of my life purpose is being a medium. That evolved into being an author because I felt guided to share the knowledge I have with others. When I was a young medium, I didn't get what I needed in books, and I want to change that. Writing about what I know then evolved into my writing fiction books. I have loved fiction and romance novels for as long as I could remember. I have always wanted to try writing one and found myself constantly searching for books that didn't exist. It was time for me to try to do something I loved and see if perhaps I could write the books that I wanted but didn't exist. Even doing something like writing a romance novel is a part of a life purpose; anything that entertains someone and takes that person's mind off his or her problems is increasing positive vibrations. Being told in a dream that I needed to write my first book, *Gifted*, has evolved into a whole new career and part of my life purpose that I love. People often ask me how I write books so fast. Other than the fact that I type fast, the answer is simple: I love it. Doing something that you love doesn't feel like work. If people buy and like my books and it provides me income, then I am being paid to do something I love.

Before I graduated college, I worked for seven years in a deli kitchen at a grocery store. Up to that point, I knew basic cooking skills. Over my years there, making everything from roasts to pasta salads, I learned my way around a kitchen. When I worked at the deli counter, I learned all about the meats and cheeses. There were times I worked in catering and learned how to make complex items. I was just working the job to do the job. It happened by accident, or so I thought at the time. What it turned me into was a good cook. I've never wanted to be a full-time chef, but I have had more than one person want to start a catering or food business with me and others that have offered to pay me to cook food or bake for them. It was something I decided not to pursue, but it may have been an option for me to pursue a career in had I chosen to. I still love watching cooking shows on television and love the ideas I get from them. I enjoy cooking and seem to do it well. This allows me to make healthy, nutritious food for myself and others. It could evolve into something more at some point if I choose it, but my love for it tells me that somehow it's part of my life purpose.

As you can see from my examples, the purpose of an Indigo is sometimes a complex answer. I have pointed out several examples from my own life along with the examples of possible life purposes. As Indigos, we naturally have lots of energy and thus can do many things to help others.

What is it that you want to do? What is it that you are passionate about? The answers to these questions are your natural indicator of a possible life purpose. Part of your life purpose is just in being here on Earth. The rest evolves as it's supposed to one day at a time. If you don't know what your life purpose is and are frustrated over that thought, then take action—any action to help others. Helping others may very likely help you receive the clarity of thought that you need to allow the next step in your life purpose to reveal itself. There's no one there telling you the answers. You can get a psychic reading if you feel you need to, but the answers are within you, whether you realize it or not. It's in the things that you want to do and in the way you feel when you are doing something you don't want to do. Do you like the activity or what you do for a living? It's a simple "yes" or "no" answer. If it doesn't feel like a simple answer—if it's not a clear "yes"—then it's oftentimes a "no." If you don't like what you're doing, then it's likely an indicator that it's not— or no longer—a part of your life purpose.

CHAPTER 10
PRAYERS AND ANGELS -
THE POWER OF ASKING FOR HELP

Interestingly, I have gone through an evolution with my religious thoughts since I have evolved into a medium. I was raised Roman Catholic and still consider myself Roman Catholic in some ways, even though I don't go to church like I used to.

For a while, I felt lost. I didn't feel like any religion wanted me. As a medium, I felt like an outcast. I never stopped believing my faith but felt it no longer fit me. Not only was I a medium, but I had been divorced. Twice. Once I began bringing dead people through, I didn't know what to believe and what organization would have me even if I did. So, for a while, I stopped praying. Organized religion didn't seem like it had a role for me any longer, and I distanced myself from the church.

After a few years of doing work as a psychic medium, it has all come back to prayer. All of those saints and angels I'd learned about as a young Catholic girl are still around me. I have realized through the readings that I give to other people that the power of prayer is amazing. I'd never stopped being Christian deep down, and it felt right to me to go back to praying. I had angels that were telling my clients to do that in my readings with them, and, when I do readings, I know that sometimes there is a message in the reading for me, as well.

If you feel you need help with your life purpose or help with raising your Indigo child and haven't already, consider praying about it. Indigos are powerful manifestors of their thoughts, whether a worry or desire, and, to someone that powerful, prayers are amazing tools.

We also have a spiritual team that is with us. You've probably heard the term "spirit guide." You may even have the idea that we all have one. We do. Indigos and lightworkers tend to have groups; I call them a team—a team of spirits, angels, our deceased loved ones, sometimes even power animals and more. We usually have a guardian angel, and we usually have several other angels around us.

The guardian angel is there to help make sure you are protected and do not do something such as have an untimely death. Other than that, our human contract with angels is that they cannot disrupt our free will. In other words, they cannot help us unless we ask. Whether you believe this is possible or not, what do you have to lose? No one needs to hear you ask—you can ask in thought—as long as you ask. You are not taking your angels away from anyone else as many of them can be omnipresent, or with several people at once. No requests are unimportant, and you do not have to be in dire need to ask for their help. Asking for their help is, in essence, a form of prayer since angels are an extension of God.

There are two primary Archangels that work with Indigos: Archangels Michael and Metatron. In addition, there are several others that I work with and will share with you.

You may find out more about these angels in my book, *Gifted – A Guide for Mediums, Psychics & Intuitives*.

Angels

Archangels are, in many ways, an extension of the hand of God. They work to carry our prayers to God and also to dispatch teams of even more angels to help answer our prayers. There are more archangels than the ones in this section, but these are the ones I feel guided to share with you and work with most often. I am listing them as a resource for you so that you can know who they are and what their specialties are. As with any angel, you may call on them for anything. This resource may help point you in the right direction if you do not know where to start.

Archangel Michael – Protector

Archangel Michael is the Universal, or all-purpose, Archangel. He shields and protects all who ask, and he has contracted with some to come as part of their spiritual team. He is often associated with police officers and any additional civil servants who protect others. He is with the Indigos, as they are warriors of some sort who effect positive change. He is also a wonderful resource for technology and issues that need a fix of some sort, such as help with your computer or a plumbing fix.

He also works to protect mediums, especially if they are "ghost busting." He can dispatch a squadron to help a lost soul heal and cross over to the light.

Color: Purple/Cobalt Blue

You can ask Archangel Michael to guard you at all times in all relationships and aspects of your life. He will make sure that you are safe. He wants you to know, however, if you do this, you may also lose some relationships or situations in your life that are not for your greatest and highest good.

These relationships may or may not re-enter your life at a time when they are better suited for your greatest good. In many instances, his intervention helps to align your energy with those that compliment it the most, and it can also bring wonderful new relationships and situations into your life, as well.

Archangel Metatron – Akashic Records, Children

Archangel Metatron is one of two Archangels who lived as mortals before becoming Archangels. On Earth, he was known as the profit Enoch. He has now ascended to the Heavens to continue his work as a scribe by recording all of the information in and for the Akashic Records. Metatron is also present on the spiritual team of all Indigo children and adults, and he is a helper to anyone that wishes to teach children for the greatest and highest good of all involved.

Color: Turquoise Blue/Green

Ask Archangel Metatron for help if you want to balance your chakras. He can do so with his sacred geometry. He starts balancing your chakras on the top of your head, with a sphere-shaped energy that contains the sacred geometry used to achieve balance.

Other Angels That Are Helpful to Know

Archangel Raphael – Healer

Archangel Raphael has green healing energy, and he is present with those that need healing or are healers. He is present on the spiritual team with all doctors and healers, whether traditional or non-traditional healers. He is also present with Crystal adults and children.

Archangel Gabriel – Messenger

Archangel Gabriel is the Messenger of God. He is present

with all orators, whether they are involved with the spoken or written word. If you are an author or musician that creates books or music, for instance, Gabriel is with you. If you are someone that speaks to crowds in an inspirational way, Gabriel is with you. Call upon him if you wish to have a child, whether through conception or adoption. He is also present with many children. This includes Crystal children and some of the Indigos.

Archangel Jophiel – Beauty

Archangel Jophiel is helpful when you need to call upon her to beautify your home, wardrobe, appearance, or thoughts. She is also a wonderful resource for clearing energy in homes. If you clear homes in any way, such as with Feng Shui, interior design, or even in helping clear Earthbound spirits from homes, call upon Archangel Jophiel for help.

Archangel Azrael – Death, Dying, Grief

Archangel Azrael is sometimes thought of as the angel of death. It is not something to fear because death is a necessary part of our existence on Earth. Archangel Azrael is always amongst the spiritual teams of mediums, hospice workers, funeral directors, and anyone that assists in the physical death process, whether it is before or after death. He also assists with grief of any kind, whether from the death of a person or relationship of any kind.

I received affirmation that I had Archangel Azrael with me when I went back to corporate America and got a job working on death settlements in the financial services industry. I already knew I was a medium, but the synchronicity is that I help dead people whether it is in a traditional or non-traditional way. The affirmation of that in my structured job was not a coincidence.

Archangel Ariel – Animals, Environment

Archangel Ariel has the face of a lion because she is known as the Lioness of God. Ask for her assistance with any issue pertaining to an animal. She can help you find the right animal to adopt or help with things such as behavior issues with animals in your life. She cares for our Earth's environment and is particularly close to anyone that feels called to work on environmental issues.

Archangel Nathaniel – Life Changes

Archangel Nathaniel has been very present with all the lightworkers experiencing life changes. He has had more presence on Earth recently, with all the vast changes that have been happening in our lives, whether good or bad. Some of these changes come to help us towards our life purpose. Archangel Nathaniel is here to help us with that transition.

I did not know that this was an Archangel I had near me until I realized that one of my favorite colors is red. I have a red car, red phone, red jacket, you name it. I have also experienced many life changes, particularly recently.

Archangel Sandalphon – Answered Prayers, Music

Archangel Sandalphon is one of two Archangels that lived as mortals before ascending to Heaven as Archangels. As a mortal, he was known as the prophet Elijah. His main role is to help carry unanswered prayers to God. He also is associated with music. When I tune into him, I often see him with a sitar or guitar. Those that play a stringed instrument are close to his cause, and all musicians may call upon him for assistance with perfecting their craft or their next musical endeavor.

Archangel Uriel – God's Light

Archangel Uriel is a very wise Archangel that is often

associated with shedding light to situations. He helps with Earthly disasters such a flood. He is known for alerting Noah to board the arc before the flood occurred. Uriel has a brilliant yellow-gold energy. Whenever I tune into this Archangel, I see him behind what looks like a silver chariot. He has amassed esoteric knowledge and can also help with divine alchemy.

Archangel Haniel – Grace

Archangel Haniel is a great holder of mystic wisdom. She can be called upon with grace in any situation, particularly something like a job interview or public appearance you may be nervous about. She has a gentle, mysterious energy and is also associated with the Moon. Haniel can help you access the information in your soul about crystals and other healing remedies.

Archangel Zadkiel – Mercy

Archangel Zadkiel helps with forgiveness. He is also known for assisting people who need to help someone else access information in their memory. He is particularly helpful with accessing the answers you already know during a test.

Archangel Raziel – Secrets of God

Archangel Raziel is a keeper of the esoteric wisdom of God. He knows all the secrets of the Universe, and he is one of the main overseers of the Akashic Records. Call upon him to access esoteric information and for help with Alchemy and Manifestation.

Archangel Raguel – Fairness and Harmony

Archangel Raguel's name means Friend of God. He oversees all the relationships between Archangels and angels. He helps add balance and harmony to relationships, and he is known for helping restore justice for the greatest and highest good of all in something such as a legal proceeding.

Archangel Jeremiel – Life Review

Archangel Jeremiel's name means Mercy of God. He often helps others review their life, whether it is a new soul that has crossed over from Earth or to help us access memories in our past from which we can learn and grow.

A Brief Note

You do not have to remember all the names of the Archangels, they are listed for you as a resource. Indigos tend to have more angels around them and are the most likely to have one Archangel, if not more, as a part of their spiritual team.

CHAPTER 11
INDIGOS AND INTUITIVE GIFTS

Many Indigos are highly sensitive. Indigos tend to be very empathic, which means that we tend to take on the feelings and burdens of others. Many times we may not even be aware of this. There are just times of the day that we just feel heavy. We may feel sad but don't know why. We may even have a headache and don't know why.

Let me give you an example. Have you ever had a job that you just hated? One of those jobs that just felt toxic every time you were at your job? I had one of those jobs. I went there every day of the week hating it, and, by the time Friday came, all I wanted to do was crawl under the covers of my bed and cocoon. I usually didn't feel better again until midday Saturday. By Sunday night, I was myself again, feeling hope for a new week. Then it would all happen again the next week. I look back at that now and think there was a good probability that I was picking up the sludge-like energy of the office and bringing it home with me; I just didn't know it.

As I've previously stated, Indigos tend to be truth tellers

and good judges of character because we have natural intuition. We may not know we are using it, but the intuition may just be a sense of knowing without us knowing where it came from. Indigos may also have gifts that go beyond the scope of natural intuition. Many are mediums, psychics or healers. They may be all of the above. They may be none of those things, either. It's not a requisite with every Indigo.

I am a psychic medium. I had no idea that's what I was when I was a kid, but I did sense that there were spirits all around me when I was a little girl. I tried to ignore the ability then because it wasn't an idea that was well-received by my family at the time, but it never went away. It was somewhat dormant while I was growing up and learning things I needed to know. One day I decided to try to develop my skills as a medium because I hoped that maybe doing so would make the dead people I felt were always chasing me go away. I later learned that all mediums are also psychic.

As a medium, I meet a good many other mediums, and I find that a lot of them are also Indigos. My clients don't tell me that they are Indigos; I'm usually the one telling them I think they're Indigos. I think it's possible that there are many Indigos with a highly sensitive sense of intuition that may sometimes go beyond intuition. When I psychically tune into the energy of an Indigo, I see an aura field around him or her that is like no other. The best way for me to describe it is that it's like an almost-navy or navy haze that covers them in addition to their own natural aura colors.

I believe we are old souls that have a wealth of esoteric information within us. We are here on Earth trying to remember what our soul already knows. We've come to use those gifts to help others, and some of us will even teach others about it.

Indigos come to Earth to help others. I remember the first time a psychic told me I was a medium. I thought he was wrong. For a long time, I fought being a medium; I thought it was a curse. How could it possibly help anyone? Later, when I started doing readings for others and connecting them with their deceased loved ones on the other side, I started to realize it was a gift that could help others.

If you are an intuitive, a medium, an empath, or a psychic, and are also an Indigo, know that you are not alone. Indigos come to Earth to help others and to lead the way for others. When I published my first book, *Gifted – A Guide for Mediums, Psychics & Intuitives*, I was scared. Scared that people would think I was nuts. That they would think my writing was crap or, worse, that my ideas were. But it was my job as an Indigo to lead the way for others. I remember being a timid, beginning medium once. I couldn't tell anyone, and my silent friend was a book when I wanted to know more about it. I wrote that book with the idea that it would be what I was looking for at that time but couldn't find. It still scared me to self-publish it, but I thought if it could help anyone it would be worth it.

Now it's a year after taking that step. There have been a few people that haven't liked it, but far more people have told me it helped them than I could have ever imagined. What if I had not followed my guidance and self-published it? The best thing you can feel as an Indigo is that you are helping someone.

What I didn't realize would happen as a result of that was that it would inspire other people that wanted to be authors to come to me and ask me how I did it. So I started blogging about my self-publishing experience and my overall experience as an author. It is humbling to know that I somehow am helping others just in self-publishing my own books, but that's an example of Indigos being leaders whether we realize it or not.

It's our job to lead the way for others. Maybe that's as a medium. Maybe it's not. Regardless, many Indigos have intuitive abilities that they've brought to Earth to share with others whether they realize it or not.

CHAPTER 12
MUSIC, PERFORMING, AND
THE INDIGO

I was born with a love for music. One of my parents was always playing records, and, as a little girl in the early 1970s, I had a little 45-speed record player. It was one of my favorite things. I could play my favorite songs and sing along to them with that record player.

As I got older, my father told me that it was better for me to listen to music than it was to watch the television. That was when I got to know his record collection; that collection contained a lot of Motown records, and, in that, I developed a love of R&B, funk, and soul music.

When rap music was born, a lot of people didn't understand it. Some people hated it. I didn't hate it; I was intrigued with it. I remember in high school my friend and I found a cassette tape called Rap's Greatest Hits Volume 1 in the drug store clearance bin. We used to drive around the town as many teenagers do when they get their license and want to exercise it just for the sake of driving. After we bought that cassette tape and listened to it while we were driving, my love of rap music began. We walked around high school chanting the lyrics of our favorite rap songs to each other and didn't care if other people thought we were nuts. I even wrote "Beastie Boys" on my jeans. It was not the only music I listened to, but my love of rap and hip hop music grew. It was never a big secret, and I was always rather surprised at the vehement dislike I would get from others in regards to rap music. For years, I judged an amateur songwriting contest, and I was one of the only judges that would take the rap category.

Rap music, to me, is one genre of music that might be on the soundtrack of the Indigo if such a thing existed. Some of that music is fueled by the anger that is inherent to the Indigo. As Indigos, sometimes we like to listen to what I would call "angry" music. A lot of rap, heavy metal, and other music fits that description in that the music being written and performed is an outlet for a voice of anger and truth, at least according to the artist.

Music is important to us, no matter what genre. It's a means of expression and, to an Indigo, it's important. If we aren't the ones writing or playing the music, we are the ones bobbing our heads to it or turning it up loud in the car as we get lost in the music.

Perhaps, there have been hard times in our lives when we have relied on music to get us by. You don't have to be an Indigo to like music, listen to music, or create music.

I'm an Indigo, and I'm also a musician. I received my first piano as a toddler, started singing shortly thereafter, and ended up in college as a music major. First I went to a large college where the music program was focused on classical music. I didn't feel classical music was what I wanted to perform but decided to go through the motions. I did fine until I had a teacher that wanted me to learn opera; I had an aversion to opera and to say I had no interest in pursuing that would have been an understatement. I ended up dropping out of that school and later went to a more contemporary music college that better fit me. There I excelled in ways that I never had in my previous classical music education.

I grew up thinking my whole purpose was to sing and play music. I now realize it's a hobby that I still love. I would bet that there are many Indigos just like me; somewhere within us, there's a musician, even if it's a frustrated musician.

Many Indigos that I have met are also musicians. Music is a great natural outlet for the powerful feelings that we sometimes keep inside, and we are able to purge some of our anger or whatever emotion we are dealing with through music.

Other aspects of performing are also inherent within the Indigo. One of my best friends is an actress; she's also an Indigo and the mother of an Indigo. We met when we were in high school. She always sang in class, and I turned around and told her to "shut up or join the chorus." She did, and we've been friends ever since.

In high school, we were in musical theater together. I liked to be in plays but felt that I usually got my small roles in productions due to my ability to sing. She, on the other hand, had it all. She could act, sing, and dance. This evolved into her love of musical theater and acting. She later worked with some of her peers to start a community theater in an area that they felt really needed a theater. Now her profession is acting and doing voiceover work for television and radio.

Indigos may be comedians, actors, or some other form of entertainer. The chaos that we grew up in made us wonderful at acting. We often had to act happy or like everything was okay in the midst of chaos. That naturally molded our ability to act. We had to act to survive. We had to tell jokes to lighten up the heavy energy around us. The skill set that we retained out of that has turned many of us into professional full- or part-time performers and entertainers.

CHAPTER 13
INDIGOS AND CAREERS

Many Indigos are self-employed. Indigos tend not to like authority figures and may have found out a long time ago that we are best as our own bosses. We make excellent entrepreneurs and may always be good at manifesting work, money, and things that we are good at as we go along and learn about life more.

One thing that Indigos excel at is leadership. We are natural born leaders, whether we like the idea of being a leader or not. People follow Indigos whether we have consented to be a leader or not. I have been a manger in corporate America for most of my adult life. I got my first manager position when my boss announced that he was leaving one day and that I would be responsible for the team when he left. I later ended up becoming the permanent manager of the team after I'd essentially been tossed into the management position. I have now been a people leader for more than 10 years, and it's something I'm good at.

Indigos don't even have to formally lead. You may do so

in your actions. Were you the first one of your friends to come out of the closet to your friends and family and lead the way for your other friends that were gay? Were you the first person among your friends to raise a child by yourself when it was not the popular thing to do?

When I wrote my first metaphysical book, *Gifted – A Guide for Mediums, Psychics & Intuitives* and clicked "publish," I was unknowingly leading the way for many others. I was leading the way for the audience reading the book that needed that information in their journey. I was also going very public with being a psychic medium and author. In both those things, I was leading the way for others. I self-published my books. I then decided to do something even more uncommon and publish in a fiction genre (romance). In doing so, I was leading the way for others who may want to do something similar. Being asked by other aspiring authors about my self-publishing journey caused me to do a series of blog articles about my journey to help other authors that will evolve into another book called *The Dream – How I Self-Published & What I've Learned Along the Way*.

Many Indigos are protectors: soldiers, police officers, firefighters, security guards, and other civil servants that protect others. Lawyers that decided to go to law school to defend others against crime are often Indigos.

When Indigos are in the wrong occupation or a career that no longer nourishes our soul, we become frustrated and/or depressed. We become frustrated because the job we once enjoyed every day we now dread. We might talk ourselves into going to it for the benefits or something similar, but, deep in our souls, we know that something is off.

It is fairly common for adult Indigos to have midlife career changes. I started working in the financial services industry when I graduated from college. I was a music major, so finance was the last place I expected to work. I found out later that musicians are often good with numbers which now makes sense to me. I quickly learned that I loved my job in finance. I was promoted a couple of times, and it energized me to be in that business. I felt good when I got up to go to work every day. For twelve years, it was my constant. No matter what was happening in my life outside of work, I had my job to go to and I loved it.

Then all of the sudden, the job became boring to me. I didn't like being a people leader anymore and often felt bad after work, not fulfilled from a day's work like I used to be. I wanted to move to another state, so I thought that perhaps if I worked for the same company in Boston as opposed to Minneapolis that maybe it would get better. When I made the move to Boston and started working for the same company, I realized I liked my job even less than I had prior to my move. It got to the point where I was leaving work on a Friday night and going right to bed not to emerge until Saturday afternoon. It was almost like I had to emotionally detoxify all the energy I absorbed all week at the office. Progressively, the job started to make me physically ill. I would become nauseous when I thought of going to work, and I started to realize I had to do something about it, so I quit. I had never done anything like that—just up and quit a job without a backup plan—but I just couldn't do it anymore. I was desperate. I needed to be free of the job for my own wellbeing.

I decided to get my real estate license after that. In Massachusetts, it only required my going to school for a weekend, taking a test, and then I was licensed. Real estate energized me, and I had the capacity to do sales. Or so I thought. It didn't end up being all I thought it would be, and I felt lost once again in regards to my career. My family teased me, wondering what I would change to next.

When I moved back home to Minnesota, I did some soul searching to figure out what to do for a career. I even told the Universe I'd be a full-time psychic medium if it was time. Apparently, it wasn't time and, after lots of searching for any job at that point to help me pay the bills, I asked the Universe for another job in the finance industry. I had done it for twelve years, I knew I was good at it, and I'd felt lost for a couple of years. I wanted the safety and structure of a job I knew I could do and would be appreciated at.

Being back at a job I knew I could do didn't satisfy me for very long. Still, I couldn't just quit without a plan. I tried that once, and let's just say that now I know what not to do with self-employment. Then one night I had a prophetic dream that told me to write a book. That led me to my first book, *Gifted – A Guide for Mediums, Psychics & Intuitives*. I knew I'd write another metaphysical book after that, but after the year of hard work to put out *Gifted* in the hopes that it would help people, I wanted to do something for me.

As a young girl, I grew up reading books. I was an only child, and, as a little girl, books entertained me when there was no one to play with. I loved the escape that a good story could give me. The love of books has stayed with me through my life. Although I'll read anything, my preference is normally romance books. I love the happy endings. I read too many Stephen King books when I was young, and they scared the life out of me. I used to fear that the character Gage from Stephen King's *Pet Sematary* was going to pop out of my closet with a knife in his hand.

I learned when I went to publish *Gifted* that I could self-publish, and that knowledge assured me that I could write anything I wanted. I had always wanted to try writing a Christmas romance and decided to try to get a book together quickly in time for the upcoming Christmas season. I had no idea if I would be any good at it, but I knew that all the reading that I had done was a first step in doing the research necessary to know what made a good romance book.

That book was *Dubicki's*. While I was writing that book, I became as entranced by wanting to know what happened next in the story as I did when I was reading a book. It was then that I knew I'd always be an author. My true love of reading is fiction, and the thought of being a fiction author is delicious to me.

I didn't expect a surprise career in addition to my being a medium, and I find that I love it. It's perfect for me. It will also help me transition into self-employment and ultimately make me an entrepreneur; being a self-employed entrepreneur is sometimes the perfect career choice for an Indigo. I still want to flip a house someday, and who knows what direction my career will take? As long as I'm doing what I love and am true to myself, abundance will follow me.

In my readings as a psychic medium, I often say, "You can't make this stuff up." Well, if you would have told me that my career would look like it does now long ago when I thought I knew what I was going to do with my life, I would have laughed. Instead, I got two new career options when I was in my late-thirties and early-forties that I never expected.

So, if you are one of those people like me that are not satisfied with your career, what is it that you want to do? If you don't know what you want to do, ask your angels for clear signs that you can easily understand. Then trust that you will be guided to the perfect career for you at the perfect time.

CHAPTER 14
GRIEF AND SADNESS IN THE INDIGO

Indigos tend to have heavy moods. We don't always laugh as easily as others seem to. Not only are we told sometimes that we're too serious, we have a hard time balancing our own emotions sometimes. Because we're empathic, meaning that we feel and absorb the emotions of others or feelings of pain that are not our own easily and without knowing it, we can walk around in a state of sadness and not know why. We are old souls that have also seen the tragedies of the Earth in other lifetimes, and we carry this heaviness in our soul. We can't explain it, but there's just a sadness that comes from within at all the injustices on the Earth, past or present.

Sometimes this feeling of sadness overwhelms us. We literally do not know what to do. Not only do we feel desperate sometimes in not knowing our purpose, we know that we cannot single-handedly stop all the injustice in this world. Some days we just want to crawl out of our skin.

As a way to cope with the heaviness I often felt, I used to

joke that I knew that I had to be strongly encouraged to come back down to Earth. I imagined myself on a nice cloud in Heaven eating bon-bons and enjoying the peace that I felt being at home in Heaven. I thought I was just here to help others and that it was a onetime deal and then I could go "home" to Heaven. Then I could "graduate" and not have to come back down to Earth again. Ever.

Then I did a meditation journey into my Akashic records. The Akashic Records are something known to contain the collective consciousness of ALL. All happenings on Earth and within the planetary system are often thought of as a library. This is how I think of them. Anyway, there I was looking at a figurative picture of all of my lifetimes, past, present, and future. When I saw what I assumed were future lives because they were out in front of the one I was living now, I groaned. I realized that maybe this wasn't my last time on Earth, after all.

Being on Earth and having a body is an advanced assignment that God, the Universe, or whatever you'd like to think of the higher power as gave to us. It's not easy to be here. As lightworkers, we have to balance our very human ego and emotions with the spiritual side of our higher self. That's not always easy.

As Indigos, we are sometimes considered fighters or stronger than someone outwardly more sensitive. Inside, though, we are almost more sensitive than those that wear their sensitivity on their sleeves. When we get angry, frustrated, or cry, the energy of that permeates more widely than we know. We are powerful souls, and this manifests itself into our humanity. Powerful energy experiences powerful loss.

When tragedy strikes us, such as the death of a loved one, we grieve so hard for so long that we may get lost in that grief. We will carry that grief with us as we move forward and that contributes to our overall sadness.

It's okay to be sad. It's okay to have a heaviness to us and to be told we're too serious. The key is to try to be patient with ourselves when we have these moments. We just have to try to master pivoting out of them. Pivoting is a term that was introduced to me by the teacher Abraham Hicks regarding the law of attraction. The law of attraction states that our energy and state of mind creates our experience. When we are thinking positively, we attract positive experiences. When we are thinking negatively or thinking bad thoughts, the best thing that we can do is to learn to pivot out of that thought and into a better feeling or thought which will allow us to more easily flow to and attract experiences that we want, to be with people or do things that make us feel better, and to know that it is safe for us to have moments of happiness.

We came to Earth to help others. We are also here to try to enjoy each moment the best that we can. They will not all be happy moments, but they will not all be sad, either. We need to be patient with ourselves if we feel like we can't laugh or can't have fun. If we feel guilt in doing that when there are so many other people suffering in the world, it might be time to take a self-inventory. It's okay for us to be happy for just a moment, for just today, or to relax for a while in whatever way that may be.

In nurturing and taking care of ourselves, we replenish our energy. When I write books, I have a tendency to stress myself out. I set goals for myself and know that I can't write fast enough sometimes. This has been particularly hard to balance with working a day job that takes up the majority of my day. I spend most nights when I come home from work writing. At some point, I promised myself that I would not miss life because I work all the time with both jobs, my day job and writing. It's hard but I have to allow myself to take nights off. I feel a sense of responsibility when I know that people are anticipating a book, but I also have to relax and take care of myself.

The other night, I was beside myself with stress. I had to come home from work and felt overwhelmed with all the tasks I had to complete in front of me. I wanted to make time to write, but I knew that in the mental state I was in it would be forced. In my experience, the material that I force usually ends up being re-written. So I took the night off. I know now that no matter how long it takes, the book will get done. My first book took over a year to write because I was not able to write every day. And still, at the end of it all, the book was published. As I sat there watching television and just relaxing, it felt wonderful. It was in that moment of appreciation for my own self-care that I knew that my readers will get a better book if I take a night or two off to take care of myself. It replenishes my energy which in turn allows me to write more effectively.

When Indigos take a moment for themselves, everyone benefits. Our energy affects the collective energy of this planet, whether we know it or not. As lightworkers, part of our purpose has been fulfilled by just being alive. We are souls having a very human experience. We are here for a reason, even if we don't know what that reason is. Now we just have to find the balance and allow ourselves moments away from it all when we need them.

CHAPTER 15
INDIGOS AND ADDICTIONS

Many Indigos have had experience with addiction at some point or another. Some Indigos may still be immersed in their addiction and not realize it's an addiction or problem, or they may still continue with behavior that they know has to stop.

My first addiction in life was to Nabisco Oreo cookies. My whole family has loved cookies for as long as I can remember. To this day, when I go home to my dad's house, there is always a jar with cookies in it. I often joke and say I could eat a cookie made of twigs and dirt. When I was a kid, I used to sneak to the cookie jar several times a day to get a handful of cookies, and, somehow out of that, a love of Oreo cookies grew. Some people like cake. Some people like chips. I like cookies.

I never thought I was an emotional eater. I had vocalized on more than one occasion that eating was a nuisance that I'd rather not have to deal with. I also said I was never going to diet. I hadn't been on a scale in years and always felt I wore my weight well, so to speak. In December 2011,

I stepped on a scale in a doctor's office and saw my weight. It was worse than I thought. I was ashamed. I knew then that I had to make a change and asked my angels to help me find a weight loss plan that would work. For me, that ended up being Weight Watchers. I lost nearly forty pounds in just over a year and would never have believed I could do it until it happened.

The hardest thing for me to give up was cookies, namely Oreos. Around that time, I bought Doreen Virtue's book *Constant Craving* which has foods listed in the back and the emotional reason we eat them, kind of like Louise Hay's *Heal Your Body* which talks about the emotional reasons we create disease in our body. When I read what it said for Oreo—the probable meaning was tension and shame, punishing oneself for perceived lack of love—it struck a nerve with me and I sobbed. I had no idea one little sentence could unleash whatever it was that I was holding within me, but I have not had a craving for Oreos since that day.

Both my mother and father were cigarette smokers. My father quit smoking when I was little, but I lived in the house with him and my grandparents and my grandpa smoked. When I was a young teenager, I started sneaking his cigarettes to try them with my friends.

By the time I was nineteen, I started smoking full-time. That meant a pack, or twenty cigarettes, a day. That continued for about seven years, and then I quit the first time cold turkey. I had quit for six years while I was married to a man who didn't like smoking. The minute we got divorced, I started smoking again. That was in 2004. In 2008, I took a smoking cessation pill which worked until I stopped taking it, and then I went back to smoking. This time I smoked less: 3-5 cigarettes a day. I had a hard time giving up those last few "emotional" smokes and told myself it would be easy to quit since it was only a few cigarettes a day. It wasn't. The few cigarettes a day continued for another six years before I quit again.

2009 to 2011 were very bad years for me. I can imagine that I'm not alone as I have had it come up in many readings that many of us, whether Indigo or not, had a hard time in the last few years. I felt like the rug was pulled out from under me. To make a long story short, the person I thought I was going to spend the rest of my life with broke up with me, which also meant I had to find a new place to live while I was nursing my heartbreak. I landed in a temporary apartment that was conveniently next to a bar. One of my girlfriend's had also gone through a breakup, and we spent a lot of the next nine months while I lived there over at that bar, drinking heavily.

Since my plans had changed with my former relationship, I began to think about the fact that I had always wanted to move to Boston, Massachusetts. It was 1,400 miles away from where I lived in Minnesota, but I figured I would be okay since I had family in Buffalo, New York, which was an eight-hour drive from Boston. Since the Universe seemed to have other plans for me, I figured I'd check one box off my bucket list in the process and move to Boston.

I had a job in corporate America most of my life, and I ultimately transferred with the same company out to Boston. I had one friend in Boston, but he didn't live close enough to me to see him all the time. No one could prepare me for the culture shock of moving like that. It may not have been a different country, but it sure felt like it. The people talked different, the roads to drive your car on were very different, and the job I took felt very different to me. A month into the move, after my initial excitement wore off, the grief set in. All of the sudden, I felt like a wet blanket had been thrown over me, and all I did was cry. It was terrible. I wasn't going to give in and go home over that, but it was tough.

That first Fourth of July—Independence Day, a national holiday in the United States—I was sad. I missed home, my family and friends. As I listlessly walked down the street in the suburb of Boston that I lived in to take the bus into the city to watch fireworks, I spotted a pub that was open. A drink sounded good since I felt so alone and was homesick. So I walked in and bellied up to the bar. I decided to have a beer to pass the time before I went into the city.

After that day, I ended up in that bar a lot. When I was lonely, it was my home away from home. I'm an extrovert, which means that I energize socially. I could always find someone to talk to me at the bar. After spending nearly every weekend in bars with the cover band I played music with for years, bars became a familiar-feeling home for me. It was the very thing I hated about being in the band, but it still contained some feeling of home to me when I was so far away from my own home. I would go to that local bar on Sundays to watch football with the other people I knew. I met friends there, even a boyfriend.

When my friend came out to visit me and we walked down the street to the bar, many people I encountered said hello to me. She said to me, "What do you mean you don't have any friends here? Look at how many people just said hello to you?" I thought, "Yeah, but I met them all at the bar." When I moved back to Minnesota a year after I'd moved to Boston for a variety of reasons, including a death in our family, I lived with my mom for six months. Those were some of the darkest few months of my life. I moved back to a place where I had no source of income. I didn't know if I was going to stay there or move back to Boston. My feelings were torn on the subject; I felt lost so I turned back to my old friend alcohol.

I had a moment when I thought, "Lisa, you did not come into this life to be an alcoholic." I had begun drinking heavily as a result of past heartbreak, and I knew that I had to leave that behavior behind me or I might actually become the person that I feared. I grew up with some clear examples of alcoholism around me, and that was not an experience I wanted to have myself.

Many of you have gone through something similar and have either overcome your addiction or know that you need to overcome it. It's natural for an Indigo to feel pain at a higher level than others. We may be the warriors on Earth, but we feel the world's pain which makes us want to fight for the causes we feel necessary on Earth. This doesn't mean it's any easier for us to endure that pain, and many of us turn to addiction as a result. I heard one of my spiritual teachers say that being on Earth is an advanced assignment for souls. I believe that. It's a heavy place to be, and somehow we just don't know any other way to handle the pain than by numbing it with food, cigarettes, coffee, alcohol, drugs, sex, or something else.

We do not come to earth to be perfect. We do come here for lessons and growth on a personal level. Perhaps the addictions that we have overcome, or learned something from, better enable us to help others in ways we might not otherwise expect.

CHAPTER 16
LIFE CHANGES AND THE INDIGO

There tend to be many life changes for an Indigo. If the Indigo is a child, one such change could be the divorce of the child's parents and/or the loss of a parent. A move resulting from the divorce of the parents can cause stress in the Indigo child. Also, the fact that the child may have to go back and forth between the homes of each parent in the case of joint custody can cause stress in the Indigo child.

Adult Indigos may have experienced divorce or a broken home when they were young. They may have also experienced other dysfunction. I did. I went into life determined to do everything "right" and not like I'd seen. Both of my parents were divorced twice by the time I was a teenager. I felt that there was no way I was going to do that. Now, not only have I now been divorced twice, but I have had other committed relationships that were like marriage. There have been times when I've wondered if there was either something wrong with me when it came to romance or that I was perhaps meant to be alone. I even thought that maybe spiritual teachers were just supposed to be alone so they could serve others. I realize now that having to be alone to serve others is probably not always the case.

As lightworkers we may simply learn our lessons faster in relationships and move on. But, just like anyone else, we all want to believe that there is one person out there that we can be with forever. We may have had our hearts broken and be afraid to be hurt again. We might tell ourselves that we'd rather be alone than to ever feel alone while in a relationship or be in the wrong relationship again.

As I've said, I have had two divorces. Those were followed by a relationship that was like a marriage that ended, too. Now I'm in my fourth committed relationship with the intent that this is IT. I trust that there is a purpose to all of this, even if I don't know what it is right now.

The relationship changes in my life have led to a lot of moves. I'd move out on my own, I'd move in with a new person, it wouldn't work, and I'd move out on my own again. Rinse, lather, repeat.

In personal relationships that are not romantic, Indigos tend to have a wide network. I can talk to almost anyone, and many Indigos also have that gift of gab. It doesn't mean that we want to talk to everyone—quite the opposite—but we can and will if we need to network for business or some other reason. Therefore I have lots of friends and acquaintances, but few of them actually know me. These friends and acquaintances know the side of them that I show them. I'm guarded. So are you. We've had our share of hurts and are not going to make ourselves vulnerable to just anyone. I have one best friend other than my boyfriend. She knows me and I know her. We've known each other since we were kids and have been friends ever since. Besides that, I have a couple of other close friends.

Adult Indigos tend to have a large network of people they know, be it acquaintances or friends, but they will only keep one or two people really close. It's not that they don't have room for anyone else; they just know that true friends are hard to come by. They've had that internal truth detector in there all along, and Indigos' inherent knowledge that people aren't always what they seem tends to keep other people out at arm's length.

In 2009, my life started to fall apart. I was in a committed relationship that I thought I would be in for the rest of my life. It didn't turn out that way. I got my heart broken. I was living in his house, and I had to find a new place to live while my heart was broken.

When I had finally moved to a transitional apartment until I made my next move, I decided to move to Boston. I had always wanted to move there. I figured I'd give it a go, following the adage that when life pulls the rug out from under you, sometimes you have to change your point of view. People told me I was nuts, the economy was this and that. By then, I knew about the law of attraction and didn't believe I couldn't live my dream just because the economy was one way or another.

I found a job in Boston, got an apartment there that was more expensive than any mortgage that I'd had in Minnesota, but did not give up. I knew I may have to sacrifice to live my dreams, but I could do it. When I got there, however, I hated the job. I quit because I couldn't breathe staying in a toxic job. I went into another career thinking it would pay off, but it didn't turn out quite as I'd expected. While I was waiting for money to come in, I spent all of my savings, my retirement plan, you name it. I was determined to stick it out. After a few months of trying to figure out how I was going to pay my bills and stressing out about my income and being far from home, I finally decided to put my things in storage and go home to Minnesota to live with my mom for a few months to regroup.

In the six months I lived with my mom, I tried to figure out why all of this was happening to me. By this time, I had woken up to the fact that I was a medium and spiritual teacher and was willing to do that, so I couldn't figure out why things were still falling apart. There were days that I didn't want to be on Earth anymore—not suicidal, but dark. To make matter worse, sometime during my year in Boston, my house in Minneapolis that I had before I left was foreclosed upon due to the downturn in the economy and mortgage crisis.

Does any of this strike a note with you? Life changes seem to be the mantra of the Indigo. We are constantly changing, and Indigos are powerful beings. Sometimes things end for us because we are creating our new reality without even realizing it. Sometimes those instances that we have had where it seems like the rug was being pulled out from under us is—particularly like the ones I have described in my own life that have taken place over the last 5-10 years—happen because it's part of what we signed up for before we came to Earth. Through experiencing these kinds of events, perhaps the energy that we do not need falls away. In our old situations, relationships or belongings falling away from us clears the energy for something new—something better. It's hard to see it at the time, and it's hard to get through.

Our souls chose these lessons even if we don't know why. We don't have to know why. We just have to hope that it makes us a better person and try not to let the anger that is so natural to us dwell in us for too long as a result of what we've gone through.

CHAPTER 17
SO I'M AN INDIGO: NOW WHAT?

Does the thought that you're an Indigo relieve you, fill you with anxiety, frustrate you, or validate you? Perhaps it makes you feel all of those emotions and more.

I had heard the term "Indigo" many times before I was ever identified as one. I never knew what it meant, but I just figured it was some New Age term to label new kids coming to Earth. I chalked it up to everything else New Age—in some realm I didn't really understand or care to understand.

That all changed the day that the spiritual teacher addressed me as an Indigo Warrior. Since that moment, I have made it a priority to learn all I can about Indigos. I started to realize how many other Indigos I knew and was around, and then I started helping them through readings that I provided. Sometimes, I would just meet people and tell them all I knew about being an Indigo because I could sense it in them. I would see all that I said start to register with them and in some ways validate these people. That eventually evolved into this book.

That's where you come in. You're an Indigo, too. You're not alone, even though it often feels like it. Sometimes I think we feel like the most "alone" people on the planet— that no one understands us and we'll never fit in. That can be overwhelming. Now you know that you, too, came here to help other people, but you still may not be sure how.

The answer is up to you. What is it that you feel passionate about? What is that dream that you've always had? What makes you mad? Take guided action towards the direction of your dreams. If you don't know what those dreams are, that's okay. If you don't feel guided to action, try to relax and enjoy the ride of life.

As an Indigo, I always feel like I'm supposed to be *doing* something. That feeling usually instills me with abundant energy to do things like write four books in a year while I'm working full-time. But I have to remember not to over extend myself, and so do you. I believe that a part of our life is to enjoy it and to take guided action towards the direction of our dreams one step at a time. The only person that can determine what that next step should be is you.

CHAPTER 18
MEMOIR OF AN ADULT INDIGO

If you have read my book, *Gifted*, there's also a version of my story in that book and how it pertains to my evolution into the life of a psychic medium. The story in this book may contain similarities because it is my life. The version of my story in this book though will be focused more on things that pertain to my being an Indigo and the evolution in my life as I came to the realization that I am an Indigo. You know what that means? My life has been through its share of challenges, and it's more than likely so has yours. I'm not telling my story in more depth to make you feel bad when you hear the challenges I have faced; I've rather written it for you, the person reading this, that may have experienced something similar. Whether it's better, worse, or different, I want you to know that you are not alone.

I was born into this world knowing that I was different. My family moved to Minnesota from New York State right before I was born. My parents talked different than the other parents. I used to ask my dad why he said "yous guys" and other phrases I never heard outside my home.

Because my parents talked "funny," or different than the region we then lived in, so did I. That later got me bullied.

My family moved to Minnesota for work; my maternal grandparents had been transferred to Minnesota. When my teenage parents got pregnant with me after my grandparents had left New York, my grandfather found my father a job at the company my grandfather worked for, and my parents then moved, too. They moved in March, and I was born in June. I was the first person in any of my family to be born in the state of Minnesota, and all I heard when I was young was how much better life was in New York, how they missed their home there, and how they didn't want to be in Minnesota.

My parents were divorced before I can remember, and, in my young childhood, they had a long, difficult custody battle over me. I don't remember that, either, but have heard about it from both of my parents and family. I am not sure of the exact year, but it was the mid-1970s. In those days, if there was a little girl, she was usually given to her mother. My parents have both told me they knew my dad was probably better able to give me a better home, but, at the time, the battle between both of my families was so bitter that they both fought for me all the harder. My mother was originally awarded custody of me but later gave custody to my father. They both decided that he was better able to provide for me at that time in my life.

I went to live with my father, and we were quickly joined by my paternal grandparents who had recently moved to Minnesota to be with us. My grandparents fought a lot, and it was stressful for me. My father always told me he loved me but was strict with his ways. I was punished a lot for mouthing off, sometimes being slapped across the face for it. I was consistently punished in the name of discipline and "spare the rod, spoil the child" until I was nearly out of high school.

I remember that I always used to see my family with a drink in their hands. When I was a little girl, I used to take sips of my grandpa's beer. One time, my great-grandma flew into town and gave me a Dixie cup full of wine to get me to go to sleep when I was hyper. I didn't know that "normal" didn't include the constant presence of alcohol until I was older.

My dad and I lived in various apartments in the city until I was about five. One night, my father heard a gunshot and decided that his child was not going to grow up in the city, so he bought a mobile home about 20 miles from the city. We lived in that trailer from the time I was 6 until I was 13.

It was after we'd moved to the trailer park that I started to get bullied. Every morning, I'd make the walk to the bus stop where all the kids that lived in that park were picked up. I held myself differently, spoke differently, and maybe the other kids just bullied me not to be bullied themselves. First they taunted me. Then they started hitting me.

I used to be terrified of going to the bus stop for school every morning because I knew the kids were going to beat me up. I hated it and felt sick to my stomach. To this day, the children's cartoon "Bullwinkle" makes my stomach flip because it reminds me of that time where I felt alone and helpless. I used to cry to my dad about it, and he felt sorry for me. He told me he used to watch me walk to the bus in the morning and cry. He knew from experience, he told me, that fighting my battles for me might give me more trouble in the long run. So he told me: "Lisa, hit them back."

In those days, my father worked the graveyard shift, overnight. Before my grandparents moved in with us, he had a hard time finding a babysitter that would take me overnight. When my father finally found a babysitter, it was the mother of the girl who bullied me the worst. When my dad drove me by to show me the house that I'd be going to, I screamed in terror and told him why. He felt terrible but explained that we didn't have any other choice, and I started going to that babysitter shortly thereafter.

Luckily for me, the babysitter had a daughter that was my age who was also bullied by the older sister that bullied me. She became one of my best friends. She taught me how to fight; she was a tough girl and later earned herself the nickname "Rambo." Once I learned how to fight back to defend myself, things got a little better for me. I was still stressed out because I was still physically fighting with other kids on an almost daily basis. By the time I was 13, I had braces and I remember being afraid of being punched in the face. I would encourage my attackers to punch me in the torso to avoid the possibility of my mouth getting torn apart because of the damage of being punched with braces on my teeth.

When I was about 13, my dad was finally able to buy the house he'd wanted for us. That drove us closer to the city, far away from where we were, and, at the time, I thought it was the end of the world. I was in junior high and felt like I was finally coming into my own. I was mad at him for moving us, but now I know it was one of the best things that happened to us.

I started a new school the fall of my eighth grade year. Everything felt so different. I didn't know it, but we were in a Jewish neighborhood. Lots of the kids asked if I was Jewish. They were all talking about their bar and bat mitzvahs, and I had no idea what that was. I felt isolated again.

Shortly after I'd started school there, one afternoon on the way out of art class, I got punched by another girl. I tried to ignore it. I didn't want to fight anymore; I was still emotionally exhausted from all the fighting that happened in the trailer park we'd lived in before. I couldn't believe it was happening there, too. A few of the tough girls called me out, and I tried to give it as little energy as possible. Eventually, it went away and I made a few friends at the new school. I still felt like I was in a bad dream and just wanted to wake up. I wanted to go home, even if I no longer knew where home was.

In those early days after we'd moved, I went to stay with one of my friends from the trailer park for a week during the summer before I entered high school. One day we went to the store, and my friend that I was with wanted to get some new makeup that she didn't have the money for. So she stole it. We had previously done some shoplifting together, but we decided it would be a bad idea to continue before that incident. When she started to put the items in her bag without paying for them, I questioned her and asked why. She shrugged and I didn't want to argue with her about it.

I knew I had done something wrong when I had stolen things before; it was something that had started when I saw some of my friends do it. It became a game to see what we could get. Those were the days of baggy pants and pockets galore on the pants, so we had plenty of places to hide things. Then we realized we could get things we didn't have the money to buy and it escalated. I always knew what we were doing was wrong, but I was tired of being "poor," which was an idea that was constantly engrained into my head by my family saying that they were broke or that we didn't have any money. So I went with the group and stole with them, and the fear I'd felt was soon replaced by the euphoria of getting what I wanted and the potential danger of getting caught.

Well, that day at the store with my friend deciding she wanted makeup, we did get caught. The minute we walked out of the store, the alarms sounded and we were both arrested. My dad had to drive to come and get me and was not happy. That happened in July. He grounded me until school started in September. I never stole again after that.

As I transitioned into high school, I made some friends at the new school and started to feel more comfortable in my new neighborhood. It was around the age of 15 that my friends and I started to go to parties where there was underage drinking. I didn't really like to drink, but I sometimes would do it because it was easier than saying no and being ostracized by the other kids. Some of the girls that were my friends were having sex. For me, that was too young to do anything sexual. I had been an unplanned pregnancy, and, as a result, my father told me about the facts of life at a young age.

One night I was at party with underage drinking. The friend I was with drank so much she threw up. She passed out; one of my other friends was off with some guy. I didn't like drinking, but I did it to fit in. That night, I had way too much to drink, and I just wanted to find a bed and sleep. I woke up still inebriated in the middle of the night because of pain. I woke up and there was a guy on top of me, entering me. It hurt. I was too out of it to know what was going on. I knew what I was experiencing was wrong, but I was afraid of what would happen if I started to cry for help. I'd been raped. It took me years to come to that realization because I knew the person that did it. In those days, I don't remember having heard about date or acquaintance rape, and I thought I had done something to deserve it. I never told my family. I was ashamed. I lost my virginity to rape. My only concern directly after the incident was being terrified that I might be pregnant. I wasn't.

I went through the rest of high school hating it. I had always wanted to be an athlete, but of my many talents, none of them were athletic. I joined the choir and the theater and the yearbook staff. I was neither popular nor unpopular. I just existed, and I found I had fun in the show choir and drama club. All I wanted to be when I grew up was a singer. I wanted a record contract, to be famous, and I wanted to get far, far away from the house and land I grew up in.

By that time, my natural anger that I had as an Indigo was continually bubbling. I was filled with adolescent hormones and mad at everything. By then we had another extended family member who had moved from the east coast and was living in our basement. The house was crowded and full of noise. Screaming matches were normal; I was an angry, vocal teenager.

After I'd graduated high school and turned 18, I felt a little more freedom. I had applied to colleges but never made up my mind, so my dad enrolled me in a nearby community college. All I wanted to do at that time was sing. The day before I was to start college, I told my dad I wasn't going. That I was going to sing. That news was not well-received, but he couldn't make me go. So he told me that if I wanted to do that, I could but that I would have to go get a full-time job and pay rent. So I did. One year later, I went to school willingly. It turned out that working a full-time job and paying rent was something I didn't feel quite ready for then.

I started attending college as a music major at the University of Minnesota in the fall of 1991. I felt a bit overwhelmed with the fact that the school was so big and that my classes were in auditoriums. The music program there was very classically-focused, which was not resonating with me. I got a lower grade than I thought I'd deserved in one of my music classes, which frustrated me because the teaching assistant was hard to understand in the large auditorium that the class was held in. By the end of the year, I dropped out of college, still not ready for or wanting that experience.

By that time, I lived with my mother for the first time I could consciously remember. My dad and I used to argue, and I ended up moving in with her for a year or so because by then she had her own house. It was a good time for us to start a healing process that we both needed from being separated in my childhood.

In the spring of 1991, I got mugged. At the time, I had a boyfriend I was seeing that lived in a really bad neighborhood in the city. My intuition was in a state of alarm right as we pulled up to the building that night. I couldn't explain it, but I just felt like something was about to happen. I talked myself right out of it, and, the minute the two of us entered his building, there was a man that maced my boyfriend and took my purse. I was nineteen at the time, and to say it scared the daylights out of me would be an understatement. For a while, I refused to carry a purse so I couldn't be mugged.

At the time, I was working at a small office supply chain in the city. I was alone in the store on a daily basis, and, a week to the day of my being mugged, my store got robbed while I was there. That completely unhinged me. I quit that job because they wouldn't transfer me to a safer neighborhood. I had a hard time with the sudden terror I felt at the world around me. I went to a therapist, and I was diagnosed with PTSD, or Post Traumatic Stress Disorder, as a result of the sudden traumas that I'd experienced. The therapist recommended an antidepressant. I didn't want to take any drugs, but the therapist pushed and I just wanted something to help my anxiety. So I ignored that bad feeling again and took the prescription. I took an antidepressant for a year and went off the drug against my doctor's recommendation. I just knew it was bad for me, and I couldn't take it any longer.

My body withdrew for a week; I shook almost uncontrollably, which confirmed my suspicion. It was a drug, and I didn't like it.

After I lost my job at the office supply store, I started working at a local grocery store in the deli kitchen. I took the job thinking it would last a few months to help pay my bills, and it ended up lasting for seven years. It was at that job that I met my first husband. I was 19 then, and he was five years older than me. The first time we went out, it didn't feel quite right. I just had this uneasiness in my stomach that I now know was a gut instinct that I didn't listen to.

After a couple of years with him, I wanted to get married and he proposed. I was married for the first time in a big Roman Catholic wedding when I was 21 years old. A month before the wedding, I started to think I was making a mistake and confided this to my father. My dad had already put a lot of money down for a big wedding, and we had relatives flying in for it. He essentially told me he understood but that I was having the wedding that he was paying for. And that was that. Down the aisle I went.

I asked my first husband for a divorce for the first time eight months after we were married. We just had nothing in common. I realized he was using marijuana, which I did not like. He had a hard time holding down a job, and I found out he had been lying to me about going to school when one day I got a call from the school wondering where he was. I wasn't making much money, yet I was supporting us both, and I couldn't handle it anymore. I started to wonder what I was thinking even getting married in the first place. Maybe I was just too caught up in the details of the wedding to pay attention to the fact that I didn't really want to spend the rest of my life with that person. I asked for a divorce again a few months later and, less than a year and a half after we were married, I was divorced. I was 23 years old. I had the marriage annulled by the church, and the Deacon that married us later told me he had reservations about our marriage and apologized to me for not saying anything before we were married.

At that time, there was still a fire burning in me wanting to make music. I was writing songs, still dreaming about a career in music, and I felt lost. I decided I wanted to go back to school and found a local school that focused on music production and performance. I started school at Music Tech, now called McNally Smith College of Music, in Minneapolis (now in St. Paul), Minnesota, in the winter of 1997. I still look back at that time as one of the best of my life. I was finally doing something about making my dreams come true, and it felt amazing. Even though I worked almost full-time while balancing the class load and school work, I was doing something for me and it felt good.

I was still working in the food service business and was becoming unhappy with working in a kitchen every day and smelling like the grease of a chicken fryer when I came home. At some point after my graduation from college, I realized I could probably get a better job. I got my resume together and started applying for more professional jobs. I didn't know what industry I wanted to work in, but I just knew that there had to be something better.

I started my career in corporate America in March of 1998 in the financial services industry, a career that would stay with me for many years. I started doing mutual fund transactions over the phone which evolved to being a people leader at some point along the way. I was tossed into a manager position when one of my bosses left, and I ended up liking it.

It was in March of 1998 that I met my second husband. I worked with him in corporate America, and we dated from

1999 to 2002, when we got married. I had a miscarriage early in our relationship. The pregnancy was an accident that was neither of us was ready for, but the day I miscarried I grieved for the child I lost. I spent two days letting myself grieve before I went back to work after that. I'd never be the same again.

When we got married in 2002, my second husband wanted to start to try having children right away. I was 29, and he was 30. He was ready to have a family. I wasn't. I went off of birth control right after our wedding in 2002. We actively tried to conceive a child with no success until early 2004. I even briefly tried fertility drugs, but other than the conception that I miscarried in 1999, I never got pregnant again. The pain of not being able to conceive started to put stress on our relationship; he didn't understand why I'd cry every month when we found out I wasn't pregnant. We went and had fertility tests and found out we were both technically normal. They diagnosed us with unexplained infertility.

As the stress mounted, we started to argue. That wasn't the only issue in our relationship, but it was the issue that caused us to break. I asked him to move out in February 2004. I had been divorced before and didn't want to fail again, so we went to vigorous counseling for the next six months. After that, we reconciled briefly but ultimately were divorced just before the end of 2004.

After that, I was done with being married. All I associated with it was the pain of divorce. At some point during my childhood, when things were beyond my control, I promised myself I would never allow myself to feel caged or be miserable again. Being divorced was hard, but being miserable in a relationship, marriage or not, was no longer an option for me.

After my divorce, I purchased a house in the city of

Minneapolis. I had saved money from the sale of our house prior to the divorce, and I wanted to buy the first house that was solely my own. The housing boom at the time would not allow me to live in a suburb close to the city as I wanted. I was not alone. It was hard for me to get used to all the sirens and activity near the house. One night, while on the phone with my dad, he asked, "Was that gunfire I just heard [on your end]?" I told him it was fireworks to placate him when, in reality, it probably was gunfire. I tried to soothe my concerns by thinking that when it was time to go, it was my time to go.

In 2005 and 2006, I felt lost. Life hadn't turned out the way I'd planned. I thought I'd have a family by then, not two divorces. I didn't know what to do next. By that time, I had a great job in corporate America. They paid me more than I ever thought possible at such a young age. I had my own house. But something was missing. I'd go to work every day, and my career would fill me up. I loved it. I loved my job. I loved my coworkers. When I got home every weekend, I felt lost.

Eventually, I started to do things with some friends that I worked with. There was a big group of us that would hang out together and play cards, and we'd drink beer while we did it. It led to other activities, but most things usually involved drinking. We'd stay out late at night on a work night, drinking more than we should on any night, let alone a work night. Yet, I loved the people I was with and liked having the acceptance of the friends I was with. After a while, they ended up telling some strange lies about me that both hurt me and distanced me from them. I realize, now, that the lies that hurt me were part of a higher plan to steer me in the right direction and away from a group of friends that were more toxic to me than anything else.

When I was no longer distracted by being out all the time, that feeling crept back again. Like there was something I should be doing, I just didn't know what. I once realized on a Monday morning that I had not talked to one other human being all weekend since I'd been at work on Friday. It was a lonely feeling. I'm an extrovert, which means I recharge socially. Sitting at home in silence is not something I enjoyed.

In 2006, I decided to get back to music. I'd grown up singing—even gone to school for it—and just because I no longer had the dream to be a rock star like I'd had when I was younger didn't mean that I couldn't get out there and perform. I started to audition for local cover bands and finally found one that was a fit. I was with that band for three years and started to miss my weekends. I was starting to miss having a boyfriend but felt like being unavailable on weekend nights was not something a guy would want.

I'd been seeing and sensing dead people around me my whole life. When I was young, I talked about it to my family and was sent to a psychiatrist. I learned to keep my mouth shut, even though it continued to bother me for my young childhood. By the time I was an adolescent, my gift as a medium was dormant. It didn't surface again until I graduated high school. I used to call my maternal grandma, Ali, because I was scared about all the things that were coming back to me. My gram had a focus on some of the New Age information that I didn't understand and helped me try to understand what was happening. She told me I was a medium. I didn't like it and didn't want to be a medium; I just wanted to figure out how to make the dead people that I felt like were following me around go away. She was patient with me and kept telling me it was a blessing to be a medium and that my soul chose that in this life, just as it chose to be a singer.

That made me mad. I knew that there was no way I chose this life. Why the hell would I choose the things that I'd been through already let alone being able to see dead people? I didn't believe in that, I didn't believe in past lives, and I didn't think I could help people by being a medium.

When I first bought my house in the city in 2005, I realized I'd always loved Boston and wanted to move there. I hadn't been sure how I was going to do that, but I started to reach out to people that lived there on various social networks. That's how I met one of my (now) best friends. We started talking on the phone, and, that first year of our friendship, thank goodness I had free long distance. We used to talk so much we barely had time to do anything else. He had hinted at romance, but I wanted nothing to do with that. It was pointless with us living so far from each other. I pushed away the thought of meeting him for a year. When I first meet him in person in 2007, we clicked. He kissed me. I told him it wasn't a good idea. As you can imagine, we started a long distance relationship. We flew back and forth for a few months and started talking about me moving out there.

At some point during that relationship, I continued to talk to my grandma Ali about all the pesky spirits in my house. My grandmother was always going to psychics; I didn't understand why. She had a party where there was a psychic medium, and he told me I was a medium. I still didn't want to hear it. He told me it was a big part of my life purpose and that music was really just a hobby for me. I wasn't sure which of those messages upset me more, but I was mad. How dare someone tell me that!

During one of my rants about the ghosts, my Grandma Ali suggested to me that perhaps I learn about how to develop my gifts by going to a psychic development class that was taught by a well-known psychic medium that lived locally. I finally agreed to it the third time she suggested it. I realized she had a point. The least I could do was go and listen and see what all this was about. I knew that the things I had been through in my life had blocked my abilities. I didn't see much on being a medium in the syllabus, but I figured it would be a start in opening back up.

I was really afraid of how to tell my long distance boyfriend I was going to a psychic development class and kept putting it off. The night before the first class, he broke it off with no explanation. I was devastated. I thought we were in love; we'd been talking about me moving out there, and he dumped me. I was sick of divorce, breakups, and heartbreak. I screamed and cried. That night I stood in my house and yelled all of my frustrations up at the ceiling to the Universe. I felt that heartbreak again wasn't fair; I couldn't handle heartbreak, and the deal was off with me doing work as a medium. I knew I was supposed to develop as a medium but thought that if I didn't get my way, I wasn't going to do what I should. That was the first time I ever heard my spiritual team speak. I clearly heard them tell me that it was fine: if I didn't want to do it, I didn't have to; but that if I chose not to, I would not be fulfilling my main purpose on Earth and that I may leave Earth earlier than I thought as a result. I had no idea if I was imagining that, but it scared me into action. I went to the psychic development class that next day.

The next day in my class, I met the third man in my life I would have a serious relationship with. Both of my husbands shared the same first name. And a last name that started with H and had six letters. This guy had the same first name as my two husbands had. And a last name that began with "H" and had six letters. When I was a little girl, long before I met them, I used to daydream that my last name was Hauser. That wasn't any of their last names, but I think it's interesting that I wanted my last name to start with "H" and have six letters. After my second divorce to a guy with the same first name, my dad affectionately told me to try to stay away from guys with that name.

When I met this third man, he had been going by a nickname that a few of his friends there had been teasing him about, and I thought that was his actual name. The last night of the class, we saw the class roster, and I saw his real name. The same first name as my ex-husbands and an "H" and six letters last name. I got home and told my Grandma Ali, and she laughed at the coincidence.

It was too late for me to stop the relationship because of his name; we already had a connection and decided to explore it. We took our time getting to know each other over the phone. He started coming to all of my band gigs as a way to get to know me, which was above and beyond what I expected. I couldn't believe the guy didn't get sick of seeing our shows, but he would just go with me and help the band load and unload band equipment. He always told me that he got a thrill out of telling people in the crowd that his girlfriend was in the band.

Very early into the relationship, we discussed having children. By the time we got together, I was 35. I was in the winter of my childbearing years and could still hear my biological clock ticking. I had been told I was normal after all those infertility tests and thought that perhaps when I met the person that I was supposed to have children with that things would change. He already had two children... and a vasectomy. I had asked him if he'd be willing to get it reversed, and he said he'd consider it. I think now it was a red flag, and I chose to ignore it.

A few months into my relationship with him, I moved in with him and his teenage daughter and rented out my house in the city. After we'd been together a year, he had a heart attack at the age of 43. One day he complained of chest pain. It never dawned on me that someone so young might be having a heart attack. I had a gig with the band that night. He offered to go with me, but I was going out of the city a long way and did not want him to need emergency assistance in a place where it wasn't readily available. By the time I left to go to the gig, he assured me he was fine. I told his 16-year-old daughter to try not to worry but to call her uncle if she saw him get worse. I called him during a break with the band that night, and he said he was feeling better. I didn't know that was because he'd taken a pain killer.

The next morning, he was still in pain, and I told him we should go to the hospital. He didn't want to go, but I threatened to call an ambulance and off we went. He kept his "I'm fine" routine going until we got in the car away from his daughter, and then he fell apart. All of the sudden, I felt like his skin took on an ashen color, and he told me to go to the closest hospital, not the one we'd been planning to drive to that his insurance covered because he thought he might die. I had never been so scared in my life.

We later found out that he his right coronary was blocked 99% by the time we'd arrived. He'd already had a heart attack, and, had we waited any longer, he would have had a massive heart attack and likely died. We were told we not only had been lucky that he survived, we were also lucky that it was not his left coronary artery—the one they call the widow maker. I spent the next few days in the hospital with him day and night, and finally he was released. After that, he had to have a stent put in his coronary artery to clear the blockage and recovered, except that he had to take several pills a day. I administered them and kept him going to the doctor.

When he had his heart attack, my dreams of having a family with him died. I just didn't know it then. A year later, he broke up with me because he knew I still wanted to have children. He told me he loved me, but he didn't want to get in the way of my having a family. Because he had a very real idea that having a heart attack may have compromised his mortality, he knew that he didn't want to have any more kids. He'd already raised two, and he was done. I was devastated.

I had to find a place to live temporarily, and my second ex-husband had a condo that he could no longer live in. He was moving on to have that family he'd always wanted, and that meant he'd have to rent the bachelor pad he'd bought when we divorced. At the time when I had found out he'd bought the condo initially after our divorce, I thought he was nuts. It was way out in the suburbs, a little too far for me, and far from where he'd grown up. Little did I know that I would love the place and the area it was in. I now joke that I think that in some ways his soul bought it as much for him as for me. Luckily, his new wife was okay with my renting from him.

I think of that condo as my healing womb. The first time I was there was six months, and it was rough emotionally. I was raw from heartbreak. Every time I thought I had no more tears, they kept coming. I had a friend who had gone through something similar, and she ended up being my saving grace. We spent a lot of time together, whether it was sitting in my kitchen making vision boards or going out for a night on the town. We will never have that time back, but I will treasure it for the rest of my life.

At some point in that period, I decided that if life was going to pull the rug out from under me again, I was going to do something I'd always wanted to do: move to Boston. I had first visited the Boston area in 2003. Since the moment of that first flight there, when I saw the airport and knew I was flying into Boston, I felt like I was home. I visited there several times over the years because of my love for the place and then later because of my long distance relationship with a man there. Every time I flew away from Boston Logan airport in the days before I lived there, I would get an emotional lump in the back of my throat because I felt like I was leaving home. I loved the home I'd grown up in, Minneapolis, but I never felt anything like I had for Boston before. With every relationship I had in Minnesota, I'd talk myself out of moving there because I was in the relationship and the other person wouldn't want to move. Well, now I didn't have the relationship that I thought was the one I'd been waiting for, and I decided it was time. I knew that I would wake up some day when I was older and regret it if I never tried it.

I spent several months planning for it: finding an apartment; a job; and purging all the items around my place that I didn't need to move long distance. It felt like it was difficult from the time I decided because when I decide I want to do something, I want it immediately like most people. In reality, it was only five months from the point I decided until I moved.

In March 2010, I left Minneapolis for Boston. It was hard for me to leave. I remember the night of my going away party. It was supposed to be fun, but everyone I loved was coming to say goodbye to me. I felt nauseous that night during the process of saying goodbye. The day before I left, my dad kept creating excuses to come over to me so he could hug me one more time. We both held on to each other and cried.

After three days in my car, I finally arrived in Boston. By the time I'd packed up my whole life and left the only place I'd known, I was sick. I drank so much cold medicine on my journey across the country that it was going to my head. I got lost trying to find my new apartment but eventually got there. I was exhausted. I was also happy. I was making my dreams come true.

I started that journey with the intention of staying there for three years. I had been offered two jobs there with exactly the same salary for the company I worked for in Minneapolis, which was my way of knowing that the choice was mine. I look back on it now, and when I chose the job I thought I'd wanted, there was that feeling in me—the discomfort you get when you know that everything seems great on paper but something just doesn't feel right about it. I pushed the feeling aside and took the job.

When I started my move, the long distance moving company told me that it would take two weeks to get my things, and I ended up missing the first day of work because all of my things had finally arrived. The next day I arrived to my new job feeling like a fish out of water. I got lost on the way to work, lost even worse on the way back, and, after having been at the same job for so long, it was humbling to be the new girl all over again.

The man I talked about earlier as the person I'd long-distance dated and I had reconciled our friendship by this point. When we broke up, I felt like I'd lost one of my best friends, and we both agreed that we wanted to stay friends after the romance ended. When I moved out there, I had the intention of living close to him. I didn't like the feel of the town in which he lived: it was too close to the city for me. I'm the kind of person that likes to be near a city but not in it. I ended up a couple of towns over from him and thought it would be no big deal. He had told me that if I lived six miles from him we'd never see each other, and I laughed it off. It turned out he was right.

About a month after I'd moved to Boston, the homesickness set in. The euphoria had worn off of being in a new place, and it was replaced by a mild culture shock. New England was so different than where I was raised. The accents they had were very different to hear all around me. I was just used to talking to my one friend on the phone, but it was surreal hearing what felt like everyone speaking with different inflections in their voice than what I was used to. Suddenly, the grief of missing home surrounded me. I was traditionally not an emotional crier, if you will, but, at that point, I could barely control the tears. I felt like I cried all the time.

The second month in my new job—that I was starting to realize I didn't really like—made it worse. I used to sneak to the ladies room and cry. By that time, I had started dating a man. It still was not enough to cure that feeling of missing home.

I was starting to feel like I hated my job. I wondered if it was possible that I was confusing it for the fact that I was homesick and just brushed my dislike to the side. A few weeks later, I thought about how my move to Boston was to live the dream not to hate my job. I had to figure out a plan. The job was becoming toxic to me. I would go home on a Friday night and crawl into bed and not feel better until the end of the weekend. Then it was time to go to work again. Something didn't feel right, but I told myself I would not make a snap decision until I took a trip home to Minneapolis to recharge myself.

I came back after that trip home with my spirit renewed. I decided I had to give the job a chance. That lasted about two weeks, and I ultimately ended up leaving the job three months after I'd started.

I had always been interested in real estate. In Massachusetts, it took less time to get a real estate license than it did in Minnesota, and the market there was a bit healthier considering the economic downturn that was taking the U.S. mortgage industry by storm. There was a healthy market there for rentals, and most people there used a real estate agent to rent. I met a broker that I really liked and went to real estate school, passed my exam, and hit the ground running.

A job in sales is very different than a job with a salary. I found that out the hard way. I was working on 100 percent commission, which I knew going in. I just thought I would do better than I actually did right away. I had a lot to learn and had not allowed myself time to learn what I needed to before I jumped head first into this new career. I ended up spending all my savings and my retirement plan to live those next few months.

Before I'd left Minnesota, I tried to sell the house that I'd bought in the city after my second divorce. There was no longer the housing boom that had forced me there, and foreclosures were becoming rampant in the section of the city it was in. I hadn't lived in it for a while, and it was vacant as I could no longer even find a renter to cover the mortgage. For a while when I'd had renters in the house, I was paying $500 out of my own pocket to cover the portion of the mortgage their rent didn't cover. I was tired of it. The house was upside down in value by then, meaning that I owed more than the house was worth. Still, I found a real estate agent that put it on the market as a short sale. We found a buyer, but I had two mortgages on the house. Since the second lien holder would gain nothing from the short sale, they wouldn't approve it.

The day I decided to walk away from the house, I had been fiscally responsible for the majority of my adult life and didn't want to default on it for many reasons. I'd tried to sell it. I'd tried to work with the banks to no avail. Now I was living in another city and no longer able to pay the mortgage, and I couldn't sell it because the one bank wouldn't approve a short sale. I shed many tears of frustration over feeling helpless about it all, but the house ultimately was foreclosed upon and was taken back by the bank while I lived in Boston. I felt ashamed about it, but I knew I'd had no other choice. I had friends that told me if losing my house happened to me, it could happen to anyone.

Around that time, my stepfather started getting sick. I'd left home hearing about the plans for the future he and my mom had, and this was not part of it. He had some fluid on his liver and had it biopsied. Ultimately, he was diagnosed with liver cancer in June 2010. It was already stage four. His treatment options were limited, and but he and my mom hoped for a miracle. So did everyone that loved him.

When I went home to visit again that September, I had the feeling that was the last time I would see him. The next few months were difficult for my mother and his family. He was deteriorating quickly. It was really hard to hear about it, being so far away and not being able to be there with them. My income hadn't been what it used to be. One of the hardest things I had to tell my mother was that I could not afford to come home to support her while he was dying. The only trip I could afford was for the funeral. He died in November 2010. I don't think my mother realized that they weren't going to get their miracle until he was gone.

I had been having such a hard time in my new real estate job, for several reasons, and started temping in administrative positions. I felt lost. I could barely pay my bills and didn't know what I was going to do. I drank alcohol a lot in that period to try to numb the pain.

My mom and grandma started to suggest that I give up my apartment and move home for a few months. I didn't want to do that. I had wanted to move out there for so long and didn't want to give up. But the more the days when by, it seemed like it might be a good idea. My grandma had told me that my mom was setting up a room for me. I still wasn't sure. Then one night I talked on the phone to my mom, and she sounded so depressed it scared me into action. I was moving in with her, if only for a little while.

I pared my belongings down to essentials. My funds were limited, and I didn't have the luxury of the full service move I had when I'd come out there. I had all of my belongings pared down to two storage pods. I stored them in Massachusetts because I figured I'd be back. Sadly, I'd seriously underestimated all that could fit inside one of those storage pods. I had to leave some things that were priceless to me on my curb for strangers to pick up. But they were just things. I had what was important and could not wait to get out of the place where I felt like my life was falling apart. I figured that my mom and I needed each other for a while.

When I got to my mom's house, I was emotionally and physically exhausted. I had cut short what had started as a dream of living on the east coast, and there I was home and unemployed because I'd left all my sources of income in Boston. I didn't know whether I was going to go back there or stay in Minnesota, but I needed to figure it out. I felt like a failure. I didn't know what I wanted, and I didn't know why I was being punished by the Universe and why the rug was being pulled out from under me.

It took about three months with my mom to decide I wanted to stay in Minnesota for good. I had made friends in Boston, but my lifelong connections were back in Minnesota. When I moved to Boston, I realized that not only were my friends and family not there, the many connections I had made in my lifetime in my home state weren't either. My Grandma Ali said to me, "Lisa, no matter how many places I've lived in, one thing I realize is that it doesn't really matter where you are: it's the people." Now I know what she meant.

I ended up living with my mom for about just over six months. In some ways, I was miserable in those six months; all I did was mow her lawn and apply for jobs all day long. I had never known what it was like to be unemployed, and suddenly I was starting to feel worthless. The one saving grace in that time was my mother. I had to swallow whatever pride I had left and allow myself to receive help from her. She let me live there for free and would give me money when I needed it. It was hard for me to do, but now I see there was a lesson in it for me in allowing myself to receive: I had no other choice. We spent time laughing and healing together.

In my quest to find employment, I offered myself up to the Universe as a full-time psychic medium if that was what I was supposed to be, but it just wasn't time for it then—probably because I was going through so much in my own life. I decided I wanted to be part of the work force again. I needed to go back to something familiar to me, and I asked the Universe for another corporate job. After having a job that I was brand new at in Boston and then being unemployed for so long, I had enough perspective to know I wanted to do something I was good at again. I knew by then I could live on a lot less money than I'd previously made. I just wanted to work somewhere that I knew the job and was appreciated for being there.

In August 2011, I started work in corporate America again. It was a different company than the one I'd worked for previously but still the same business. I managed a small team that worked on life events, mainly working with the finance accounts of people that died. I laughed at the fact that since I was a medium, it seemed to be the Universe's way of saying "You're going to work with dead people one way or the other."

Right after I started working again in 2011, I moved back

to my ex-husband's condo I'd been in before I had left for Boston. I initially didn't think that would work, but suddenly the synchronicities aligned, and I was able to move back there. I had my belongings shipped back from Boston and started the process of reconstructing my life. Since I'd sold most of my furniture before I moved, I had an apartment full of secondhand and hand-me-down furniture, but it was mine—deliciously mine.

I had always been a person who had never really believed in diets. I was neither skinny nor fat and, for the most part, comfortable with myself and the fact that I had some curves. I had always eaten whatever I wanted and did what was likely emotional-eating when I felt like my life was falling apart around me. I started to feel like my clothes were getting tight and knew I had gained enough weight that I would have to do something about it before it got out of control.

In December 2011, I went to the doctor's office and stepped on the scale. I had not kept a scale around me for obvious reasons, but when I saw the number I was ashamed. I knew I had to do something to lose weight, but I didn't know what. I prayed about it and decided that after the holiday season I was going to join a weight loss program.

The next month, I went and joined Weight Watchers Online. I paid for three months and thought that if I didn't succeed, at least I was putting a foot in the right direction. I was at the point where I felt like I could gain weight just from looking at food, so to say I was skeptical at the thought of a program that worked would be an understatement. Still, my mom had been on it, and she said that if I could make it through the first week without eating my arm off, I could succeed.

That first week was awful. Then I stepped on the scale and

had lost eight pounds. My eyes nearly popped out of my head. I didn't expect such a big number. That gave me the will to keep going. My weight loss goal was around 35 pounds. At some point in my weight loss journey, I decided I wasn't going to be miserable and miss life because of it, even if it took me longer to reach my goal. It took a year to reach my goal, and I have kept the weight off in the years since.

A few months after I'd moved back to the condo, I started to wonder what my purpose was now. I was lonely, but romance was one of the complexities of life I didn't seem to have much success with. That dream I'd had of having a family had never panned out, and I started to wonder if I was just supposed to be alone.

The place I lived next door to had live bands, and I sated myself with going out to see the good ones. When I got back to town, I had received an offer from my old band to come back, but I wasn't ready to do that yet.

I called a friend of mine in the spiritually-enlightened community. We created a group that met as a source of support for psychics, mediums, and the like since it seemed like there wasn't anything else like it. We decided to host a group on Tuesdays where we would discuss one topic of interest and come together to talk and answer questions that people might have, whether they were just opening up to this side of their lives or experienced in the field. Eventually, I started doing readings again on a part-time basis. I still felt like something was missing.

I hadn't had a serious boyfriend in a while and started to wonder if that's what I wanted again. I never wanted to get married again, but I did want a committed relationship. I started saying positive affirmations to manifest my soul mate, not knowing whether or not it was what I really wanted when I did.

Because I knew other musicians, sometimes when I saw bands I would talk to the people I knew. I reconnected with a guitar player I'd had an attraction to before I'd left. I always had a strict "I don't date musicians" rule because of the things I'd seen with other musicians in relationships and with groupies, so to speak. I decided to make an exception for this guy when I was out at one of his gigs early that summer and the spark was rekindled. That lasted for about a month, and I'll spare you the details. I found out the precise reason I'd had that rule not to date other musicians. I was angry; I got in touch with my inner romantic cynic and decided that romance just wasn't worth it and that I didn't seem to be cut out for it.

I met my current boyfriend in July 2012. In February 2012, I met a lady that gave me a cold reading and told me all about the guy I would meet that I'd spend my life with. I brushed it off. The night I met Luis, my boyfriend, I was out watching a band. I needed to go outside to get some air and went out back to the patio bar to sit down for a breather. Luis was in the seat next to me. When he tried to engage me in conversation, I immediately tried to deflect it. I was tired of the fact that there always seemed to be some drunk guy with a pick-up line, and I wasn't interested in hearing another cheap pick-up line. Still, he gently persisted. We talked for hours and ended up staying until the early hours of the morning when the bar closed. We said goodbye and he tried to kiss me and to get my contact information. I said no to both. I still was not sure because we'd met at a bar but afterwards regretted my decision. I really liked him. Frustrated with myself, I had to trust that if I was ever supposed to see him again, I would.

A few days after that meeting with the man that is now my boyfriend, I had a prophetic dream. In the dream, I died. It was so real. It felt like every near-death experience I've ever heard about. It was like I was seeing myself laying there in my bed and feeling my soul rise out of my body.

There was a gold light coming from the ceiling, and when I got near it, I felt peace and love like nothing I'd ever experienced in this life. Why would I NOT follow that light? As I looked down at my bedroom and saw myself laying in the bed and my kitties next to my body, something struck me about the experience, and I said to whomever would listen, "I'm not ready to leave yet." All I heard was a booming authoritative voice in response that said, "Then WRITE THE BOOK."

Wow. I'd always been thinking of writing a book and had put it off. Writing a book seemed a daunting task, but that put me into action. I wasn't ready to leave Earth.

That Saturday night I decided to go to the place I'd met Luis the week earlier. I had been thinking about him all week and had to see if he'd be there. When I got there, I bumped into the lady I'd met months early that had given me the cold love reading about the guy I would spend my life with. I hadn't seen her since that day and there she was! I realize now it was not coincidence. We chit chatted for a while, and I forgot all about looking for the guy I'd met the week prior for a while. Later, I decided to walk out to the patio for a breather, and there he was. He'd come back to look for me, too. The rest, as they say, is history.

I realize now that woman that gave me the cold reading months before about the man I would meet had predicted these events—Luis was the guy she described. And she was there the night we established our relationship. That could not have been coincidence. I've not seen her again after that.

When I met Luis, he told me he owned a house and where it was. I immediately said, "I'm NOT moving there." It was in the neighborhood I'd spent my formative years getting bullied, and I wanted nothing to do with it. It was not even two blocks from the school where I was bullied.

You could hear the kids in the school yard sometimes when the windows were open. I suppose I came back to the area that it happened to heal the hurt on a soul level because it's too uncanny to just be a coincidence. A year after we'd met, I moved in with him near that school I'd been bullied at.

At some point in all of this, I was first identified as an Indigo. I wanted to put the information about Indigos in my first book, *Gifted*, but I decided that it should be its own book. And that brings us here, to my present and this book.

There have been times I've thought that we need a collective support group for lightworkers. Generally speaking, among many of us there seems to be more marriages, divorces, relationships, breakups, moves, addictions, tragedies… you name it. Is it because we came to Earth to work through some things and then teach others with our experiences? I think it's entirely possible.

If you would have told me five years ago that I would be an author now, I'd have thought you were joking. After the dream and the release of *Gifted* a year after that dream, I was going to start this book. But in my heart of hearts, I had always wanted to try writing a romance novel. I released *Gifted* in August 2013. After that, before I started work on another nonfiction book, I decided I wanted to try writing a romance novel for release at Christmas. I did this while still working a full-time job during the day.

Once I started writing *Dubicki's*, my first fiction romance, I realized how much I love writing fiction. It nourishes me in a way I can't explain. I love it. Since I knew how to self-publish, I self-published that book and the second book in that series. *Indigo Warrior* is my last planned metaphysical release, for a while at least. If I feel guided or start to hear from you, my readers, what you'd like me to write about it,

I will take it into consideration. I'm going to join the Romance Writers of America soon, which is pretty much a dream come true. Some of the authors I idolize belong to that organization. I never saw this coming, but I'm happy that it did. It brings me a level of satisfaction with a career that I haven't had before. It was my "surprise" career that I now love. Between that and being a medium and my life with boyfriend and our kitties, I'm content.

I still have days when I wake up angry, frustrated, and the like, which reminds me how truly Indigo I am. I want to be self-employed but am not yet there. My guides have told me I would not be there at least until I finish this book because I need the frustration it provides me to write the book. I can almost hear them laughing as they reveal that, but it makes sense. They're probably right.

Before we part, I have something to say to you my dear readers: please follow your dreams. Write that book. Make that move. Leave that relationship. Adopt that baby. Even if people might think you have lost your mind, you have to follow your truth. If the thought of doing something brings you joy, it's a great sign that you are doing the right thing.

BIBLIOGRAPHY

- *Indigo Adults* by Kabir Jaffe and Ritama Davidson

- *The Idiot's Guide to Indigo Children* by Wendy H Chapman, Dir., MA in Ed. Psy., SRMT and Carolyn Flynn

- *The Care and Feeding of Indigo Children* by Doreen Virtue

- *Ask and It Is Given* by Esther and Jerry Hicks

- *Constant Craving* by Doreen Virtue

ABOUT THE AUTHOR

Lisa Andres has been both an Indigo and a medium all of her life. She started giving readings to others in 2009 and writing books in 2012. A prophetic dream led her to write her first book, *Gifted – A Guide for Mediums, Psychics & Intuitives* which has been an Amazon bestseller since its release in 2013.

When she's not writing, Lisa loves reading books, all things New England, a few trashy reality shows, and good conversation. She lives near Minneapolis, Minnesota, with her boyfriend and three cats.

BOOKS BY THIS AUTHOR

Metaphysical

- *Gifted – A Guide for Mediums, Psychics & Intuitives*
- *Indigo Warrior – A Guide for Indigo Adults & the Parents of Indigo Children*

Romance

- *Dubicki's*
- *Guarded Heart (Book 2 of the Dubicki's Series)*

Lisa plans to release *The Dream – The Story of How I Self-Published & What I've Learned Along the Way* in the fall of 2014, and her first paranormal romance, as well as the third book in the *Dubicki's* series, in 2015.

CONNECT WITH LISA ANDRES ONLINE

Website:
http://www.lisaandres.com

Author Fan Page:
http://www.facebook.com/LisaAndresOfficial

Psychic Medium Page:
http://www.facebook.com/lisajandres

Twitter:
http://twitter.com/lisaandres

Instagram:
http://instagram.com/lisajandres

Special Bonus

A Note from Lisa

and Bonus Chapters from

Gifted – A Guide For Mediums, Psychics &

Intuitives

A NOTE FROM LISA

Dear reader,

As I was writing this book, I began to think of my journey as an Indigo and how that correlated with my journey as a medium and psychic. I know some of you may be on a similar journey, therefore I felt that some of you may find the following information helpful paired with this book. Since Indigos can also be mediums or psychics, I have included two chapters from *Gifted - A Guide for Mediums, Psychics & Intuitives* on how to identify if you may be a medium or psychic. I wish you well on your journey, and I am glad that we have found one another.

Namaste,

Lisa

HOW DO I KNOW IF I'M A PSYCHIC
OR AN INTUITIVE?

Do you relate to the word *empathy* or *empathic*? Have you always felt that you can absorb the emotions of others, for good or bad, and it's excruciating to sometimes be in strenuous emotional situations as a result? Does being empathic sometimes feel as if it drains your energy?

You often seem to notice that people have always been able to confide their deepest, darkest secrets to you. You don't know what it is about you and have thought it must just be a vibe you give off. You are likely in a profession known for listening to others problems, such as a therapist or even a bartender. Maybe you've even joked you should be one.

More than once you knew the answers ahead of time, like who was about to call when you picked up the phone. You've joked, or someone else has, that you *must be psychic*.

Sometimes you just seem to be on a roll guessing things of no consequence, such as a baby pool at work (when the baby would come, etc.), or who was going to make it to the basketball final four. You always just seem to know what song is going to play before it plays.

You probably have had a hint of intuition more than once that you didn't listen to. You may have thought to yourself more than once, "I should have listened to my hunch and taken a different road to work," when you are sitting there in traffic because a traffic accident has now caused an unexpected delay.

Have you always had the uncanny ability to read people or just been a really good judge of character? You don't know how you know, you can just know. You're always right, no matter how others may disagree with you or no matter how long that validation takes. Not that you really needed the validation. You knew you were right from the get-go.

Throughout life, you have likely been impatient with a traditional classroom setting. It was not because you didn't want to learn, you just always felt smarter than the teachers or knew what you needed to learn did not exist in that classroom setting.

You likely have a fear of coming out of the Psychic Closet. It's scary to think of what your family and friends might do if they knew. The thought of the Salem Witch trials gives you the shivers. This is likely because your soul knows of a time when others (maybe even you) were persecuted for those gifts.

The good news is that now you live in a time where you are SAFE. You were born to do this. You came here to help others with the gift of your psychic, intuitive, or empathic senses.

If you have nodded your head in agreement at several of the things I have mentioned, then you are, indeed, psychic, intuitive, and/or empathic.

HOW DO I KNOW IF I'M A MEDIUM?

Have you always felt intrigued by the thought of mediums or ghosts? Have you had moments in your life where you think you saw a spirit or even just a flash of unexplained movement out of the corner of your eye?

You probably have always just *known* that there were ghosts near or around you. You may feel a chill, goose bumps, or tingling that is reminiscent of the hair standing up on your arms or back of your neck. Sometimes you may feel a sensation such as a sudden spot of cold air in an otherwise warm room. You may sometimes smell something out of thin air, like a smell that you used to notice on someone you knew, a perfume your grandmother used to wear, or the smell of a cigar that your father used to smoke.

You are somewhat obsessed with the paranormal. You watch all of the ghost hunting shows or anything you can find about ghosts, mediums, or anything paranormal. You cannot get your hands on enough about mediums or ghosts and are always seeking a new book that tells you something you did not know before. You always wish for another book that answered the questions that the last book didn't.

The thought of ghosts probably intrigues you and probably also terrifies you sometimes, too. What you DO know is that it always feels like there's just something else there. You may still sleep with a nightlight on or leave the TV on all night because you sense there is something or someone in the room with you. You may even dread the thought of going to sleep or getting sleepy because you seem to notice more paranormal activity at night, particularly in bed. And the thought of opening your eyes from sleep in a pitch black bedroom is scary because you never know what you will see or feel in the room with you. It's highly likely that you feel like no matter what you do, there are always ghosts around you. You absolutely cannot believe that you keep buying ghost-infested homes. Everywhere you go there are ghosts; you just can't seem to get away from them. Why?

You have always just known you were different. If you told anyone about the fact that you might see or sense ghosts, they'd surely lock you up or think you insane. You have tried to ignore the fact that you were a medium, but somehow the spirits always find you and pester you anyway. Sometimes you feel like they just KNOW you can sense them and will go out of their way to do things that get your attention. You can tell they're near when the hair on the back of your neck stands up or you get goose bumps. You probably argued with or denied to anyone that you were a medium. You may have said, "That's crazy!" and denounced mediums in some way.

If you have just read this passage and nodded in agreement at many of the statements, cried tears of relief that someone else understands, or exclaimed, "Yes! That's me!" to any of the statements, then you are a medium. You agreed to come to Earth to help others with your gift. You are one of the few special souls that have the capacity to connect others with the loved ones that they so dearly miss.

I used to wonder how the heck I could help with this gift, and I would SCREAM at anyone who tried to tell me I was a medium. I thought it was a curse. Later, when I saw how much I helped my clients, after a reading by using something I had been able to do my whole life, I realized it was a special blessing to help another with my work as a medium.

So whether it thrills you or scares you, whether you feel it's a blessing or a curse, you are indeed a medium. And you are very needed on Earth right now. You do not need to be perfect to help others. You are loved, you exude love, and you are perfect just as you are right now. Everything will happen exactly as it should, so trust that Heaven has heard your prayers and your concerns. The time is now for you to open yourself up to this gift.

Exclusive Sneak Peek

Gifted - A Guide For Mediums, Psychics &
Intuitives, Second Edition

PROTECTION AND CLEARING

Protection

It's a good practice to always ask for protection from God, Spirit, or the Source that you believe in or feel guided to. I most commonly call on Archangel Michael and the goddess Isis for protection. I ask Archangel Michael to guard and protect me in all that I do. I may ask angels to go to the four corners of my house and protect it and keep it safe, and to also do that with my car, my work, and the same for all of my loved ones.

Free will is a factor when trying to send protection to others, so you may want to say, "I want to send this person angels for whatever it is he needs," or "I want angels to protect my friend, with his soul's permission." The client may not consciously know or be ready to hear it, and you then are doing this with integrity by knowing you are not doing anything without permission.

Clearing

My favorite way of clearing is the kind that doesn't require any human tools. It is by intention and asking for help from the Angels. I usually ask Archangel Michael to come in and to clear the energy in a room; I ask him to cut the energetic cords of fear in the room and to vacuum the room and fill it with light. In addition, there are things that you can use to clear a space of negative energy such as sage, palo santo wood, Florida water, or candles.

Sage you can usually find loose or in a stick. You usually want to light it and then blow it out, leaving the smoke to go to the areas where you want to clear the energy. You may also use a fan of some sort (many use feather fans) to help circulate the smoke. It will naturally cleanse the negative energy.

Palo santo wood works in the same way. It just smells a bit sweeter and is sometimes called sweet palo santo wood. It has been used since ancient times, originating in Peru, to cleanse negative energy.

Florida water is a citrusy type of cologne water, and some believe its use stemmed from the fountain of youth. I pour some in a spray bottle and dilute it with water. You can use it as it is or dilute it as much or as little as you want. It has a very high vibration, so even watered down it's still very effective at cleansing negative energy. I use it as I feel guided, as should you. It comes in handy in an instance where it's not appropriate to have the smoke of sage or palo santo. I most commonly use it in instances where I am in someone's home doing a clearing or reading.

Candles can be used in cooperation with any of these tools to increase energy in a room. Get any scent you feel guided to, or connect with, because it is likely that your energy works in cooperation with that scent. I find it particularly helpful to have at least one candle lit when I am doing a reading for a client.

You can use any of these tools, and if you don't know

where to start, seek them out at a local store or on the internet and see which one you feel most guided to. There is not a right or wrong: it's what you feel is right for you and your personal space or practice.

Mirrors

Mirrors have an energy that can act in one of two ways. It can attract negative energy, or it can deflect it. For instance, I usually don't keep mirrors in my bedroom because I believe that they can channel and keep negative energy in the room.

I do, however, use mirrors as a means of protection, if you will. When I lived in an apartment, I put a pocket-sized mirror facing down in the bedroom under my bed, to deflect any negative energy that might come from the apartment below me.

I also carry a pocket-size mirror facing the outside of my purse (inside my handbag) to deflect the negative energy that might happen from being in crowds and being around other people. I have even seen necklaces with small mirrors facing out as a means of protection that you can wear on your person.

Crystals

In my first psychic development class, I remember everyone there was talking about crystals. They carried them with them in their pockets or handbags, kept them in between their mattresses, you name it. Even when I helped my grandma move, she had a heavy box of what she called her "good crystals." I remember thinking, "Huh? They're rocks."

The first time I received a healing with a crystal, or rock as you might call it, I was in Hawaii. There was a spiritual shop there with crystals, and when I walked in, the woman offered me a healing with an angelite crystal. I didn't know what that was, but it sure felt like it cleared me.

That opened me up to the healing power of crystals. I would go to shops that had crystals and just grab the ones I felt guided to; I didn't need to know why. Then I bought a book to tell me what some of the crystals were and about their healing properties.

I started to keep some crystals that would help me deflect negative energy. Now I have become one of those people that carry rocks in my handbag and have them in my home, too. I have some that I have no idea why I have them, but I know that it feels better for me to have them. I love agates; I always have one on me and hold one to ground me when I am giving a reading.

You may want to look into something like *The Crystal Bible* by Judy Hall as a resource to use crystals as a means of protection, for clearing, or more.

Printed in Great Britain
by Amazon